Studies in
Writing & Rhetoric

IN 1980, THE CONFERENCE ON COLLEGE COMPOSITION AND COM-munication perceived a need for providing publishing opportunities for monographs that were too lengthy for publication in its journal and too short for the typical publication of scholarly books by The National Council of Teachers of English. A series called Studies in Writing and Rhetoric was conceived, and a Publication Committee established.

Monographs to be considered for publication may be speculative, theoretical, historical, or analytical studies; research reports; or other works contributing to a better understanding of writing, in-cluding interdisciplinary studies or studies in disciplines related to composing. The SWR series will exclude textbooks, unrevised dis-sertations, book-length manuscripts, course syllabi, lesson plans, and collections of previously published material.

Any teacher-writer interested in submitting a work for publica-tion in this series should send a prospectus and sample manuscript or a full manuscript to the NCTE Coordinator of Professional Pub-lications, 1111 Kenyon Road, Urbana, IL 61801. Accompanied by sample manuscript, a prospectus should contain a rationale, a defi-nition of readership within the CCCC constituency, comparison with related publications, an annotated table of contents, an esti-mate of length in double-spaced 8½ × 11 sheets, and the date by which full manuscript can be expected. Manuscripts should be in the range of 100 to 170 typed manuscript pages.

The works that have been published in this series serve as models for future SWR monographs.

Coordinator of Professional Publications, NCTE

Audience Expectations and Teacher Demands

*Robert Brooke
and John Hendricks*

WITH A FOREWORD BY VICTOR VILLANUEVA, JR.

Published for the Conference on College
Composition and Communication

SOUTHERN ILLINOIS UNIVERSITY PRESS
Carbondale and Edwardsville

Printed in the United States of America
Edited by Timothy Burns
Designed by Design for Publishing, Inc., Bob Nance
Production supervised by Linda Jorgensen-Buhman

Library of Congress Cataloging-in-Publication Data

Brooke, Robert, 1958–
  Audience expectations and teacher demands.

  (Studies in writing & rhetoric)
  "Published for the Conference on College Composition
and Communication."
  Bibliography: p.
  1. English language—Rhetoric—Study and teaching.
I. Hendricks, John, 1953–   II. Conference on
College Composition and Communication (U.S.)   III. Title.
PE1404.B75   1989   808'.042'071173   88-31210
ISBN 0-8093-1514-9 (pbk).

92 91 90 89   4 3 2 1

The paper used in this publication meets the minimum requirements
of American National Standard for Information Sciences—Permanence
of Paper for Printed Library Materials, ANSI Z39.48-1984.   ∞

Contents

vi   Contents

Foreword

Victor Villanueva, Jr.

WRITING IS A SOCIAL ACT. THIS THEME UNDERLIES EVERY PAGE OF *Audience Expectations and Teacher Demands.* In keeping with a social perspective, Brooke and Hendricks employ a naturalistic research approach, draw from theories of critical education, and rest on insights provided by social psychology. At issue is the contradiction inherent in requiring students to write to audiences other than the teacher when students and teacher alike know that it is the teacher who will actually read and assess the students' writing. The research is less on writing as an act than on how students work their ways through the conflicts presented by a teacher's demands and the conflicts posed by a teacher's multiple and not always complementary roles in the classroom. This study examines students' experiences.

The research is also about a teacher's experience. In the pages that follow we will read about a teacher recently admitted into the academic discourse community. We rarely read about the novitiate from a pedagogical perspective (as opposed to an administrative or a political perspective). In this case the teacher is Robert Brooke. At the time of this study (1983) he is a doctoral candidate preparing a dissertation in composition theory, working his way through academic audiences, and learning of the constraints imposed by doctoral committees and readers of professional journals. His efforts at conveying this heightened awareness of audience constraints to first-year students will be examined, and we will look at his efforts at accommodating various theories of composition without becoming uncritically eclectic—his efforts at containing Aristotle, Elbow,

Flower, Lauer, Lunsford, Young, Becker, and Pike within an audience framework.

Some of this diversity was externally imposed, thereby limiting Brooke's autonomy. Part of his syllabus was institutionally mandated, required by the Minnesota writing program. The program joined elements from *The four worlds of writing* and *Rhetoric: Discovery and change*, two theoretically diverse texts. Brooke borrowed from conventional composition courses, using student notebooks, workshops, and regular student-teacher conferences. He used a portfolio-like approach for the final grade. Along the way to the final, Brooke graded on what a paper might receive if submitted unrevised—on how well a paper displayed an understanding of "the point of the assignment," the underlying audience concept. In other words, Brooke used split grading, but instead of the traditional content-form split, his was more an audience-style split. For Brooke, understanding the concept of audience would lead to an understanding of form. In his efforts and experiments we are made to consider and reconsider our own successful and less successful efforts.

If much of Brooke's course strikes us as basically conventional (and thereby applicable to most of our composition classrooms), we will find his assignments were not; they were the experiments, all geared toward a recognition of the constraints various audiences impose on writers. The first assignment relied on case approaches, in which students write to a fictional audience and the teacher pretends to be that audience in his comments on the writing. Brooke's particular twist was in having students describe the same subject to radically different audiences. The second assignment had students analyze how particular social settings elicit different linguistic forms. So that students would not miss the point, Brooke had them attend a midnight showing of the *Rocky Horror Picture Show*—a highly specialized speech community, to say the least. The third assignment had students relate a single subject in three distinct forms: traditional outlines, Flower's issue trees, and Elbow's collages. The last two assignments had students write a proposal for a paper directed to an office within the university bureaucracy that could grant course credit for that paper; students then wrote the paper. The first three assignments demonstrated the relation of text to context; the last two applied that relation to academic settings.

The degree to which these assignments "worked" is not presented in terms common to research reports. Rather than presenting developing drafts of student papers reflecting a growing understanding of the concept of audience, success or failure is discussed in terms of students' acceptance (or rejection) of teacher demands. We are shown one student's paper, but only as an example of the "teacher commentary-student revision" process. Perhaps Brooke and Hendricks originally intended the usual documentation of a successful pedagogical approach to teaching about audience, but as they tell us, Brooke grew troubled by the degree of antagonism some students exhibited by the end of the course, and both Brooke and Hendricks became confused by students' frustrations. This confusion arose from their acknowleding that the course was not inordinately demanding. Students generally did well by the end of the course, by and large having successfully complied with teacher demands; they had had many opportunities to improve their grades along the way; what is more, they had been allowed a great deal of leeway in the forms their final products could take—from standard student paper manuscript form to pamphlets and even posters.

In their analysis Brooke and Hendricks try to make sense of this student frustration by looking to theories of human development, thereby demonstrating a recognition that most of our first year college students are in fact adolescents. This is not to say that they treated their students like children. None of us should, we know. It is to say that while our sociocultural norms and our students' senses of integrity demand that we regard them as adults, they have not quite arrived at adulthood psychologically—including cognitively. Recognizing this dissidence between the cultural and the developmental partially explains the problems one might have with some of composition's applications of cognitive psychology. For the most part composition has looked to Piaget's basic works, which have children reaching cognitive maturity in early adolescence. This has led some in composition to contend that less capable first year college writers—particularly basic writers—are operating under a cognitive deficit. But as Robert Bergstrom has noted, Piaget and Inhelder's later research places later-adolescent American youth in a transitional stage between the concrete and the formal operational stages of cognitive development (Discovery of meaning: Development of formal thought in the teaching of literature. 1983. *College English* 45:745–55). Vygotsky, too, places scientific-concept formation at later adolescence (see page 80 of *Thought and Language*). We should not, then, be concerned with cognitive deficits; we should, rather, concern ourselves with culturally determined levels of cognitive maturity, recognizing American youth as different from French children from past generations. Brooke and Hendricks apparently appreciate that students are still maturing. Their approach to what they recognize as both social and psychological is to look to social psychology.

Specifically, they turn to theories of identity posed by Erving Goffman, R. D. Laing, and Erik Erikson, in which identity is seen as being constituted by way of interactions between individuals and the social contexts of which they are a part. Goffman, for example, sees identity formation in terms of others' classification of an individual on first contact, on the physical characteristics or biographical data that further classify, and on the self that is presented to others to indicate membership in a particular group. In terms of the first year student, she is coming in contact with new people and new types of people (college professors, students from other cultures and countries, older adults as students, etc.); she is finding new groups to belong to (college students in general, dormies or frat rats or ROTCies, etc.); and she is coming to regard herself differently (often reflected in experiments in dress). Her self is still forming, still shy of the comfortable, informed integrity that can accommodate (even if not accept) different world views—the rhetorical stance most rewarded by the academic-discourse community, the rhetorical stance that demonstrates an appreciation of differing audiences. In the process of forming she will try to hold on to her self-perceived identity, defined in part by the groups to which she belongs or the groups she would align herself with, negotiating her way through the conflicts posed by the various groups.

The conflict that most concerns Brooke and Hendricks is that posed by a teacher's demand that students write to audiences who will neither read nor assess their work, while the students simultaneously pretend the person who will in fact assess their work is not the reader. This complex set of conflicts is, we are told, imposed in part by the institutional setting. Classroom constraints compel the teacher not only to pretend to be a non-teacher audience but also to take on other roles in relation to students: fellow writer, evaluator of students, and student animator (to borrow Paulo Freire's term), prompting students to considerations that might foster more mature thinking. The messages the students receive from the teacher can affect how they negotiate their ways through larger contextual conflicts, as in the conflicts involved in trying to decide if they are suited for college or if college suits them.

Brooke and Hendricks address matters of institutionally imposed constraints by turning to an educational theorist who will complement, to some degree, the social psychologists whom they invoke. They turn to Henry Giroux. However, since theirs is not a critique of educational institutions, Brooke and Hendricks do not explicitly address the ideological issues that are at the heart of Giroux's theories.

Giroux's presence is nevertheless felt. For instance, Brooke and Hendricks focus on four students, trying to examine possible causes for each student's expressed attitudes toward the course and the teacher. The researchers' explanations use terms that can accommodate both psychology's identity theory and education's resistance theory—"conflict and negotiation." Yet, implicit in each student's case is an instance of Giroux's terms of opposition, accommodation, and resistance. Susan and Kris resist Brooke's demands, believing them either idiosyncratic, and thereby not generally applicable to writing for college, or else confusing. Each of these students rejects, to some degree, Brooke's concepts but each nevertheless complies with his demands. Doug opposes. But as Brooke and Hendricks portray him, his is a rather charming opposition: claiming to like the teacher and claiming to understand the teacher's concepts but asserting and displaying a complete lack of interest in writing. George begins the course by resisting but later comes to accommodate the teacher's demands, accommodating to the point of becoming the teacher's advocate during discussions with other members of the group. Brooke and Hendricks explain these student negotiations in terms of the students' self-perceived identities, defined in part by their membership in or alignment toward particular groups, especially their membership among the community of first year college students.

Brooke and Hendricks, then, are concerned with individuals as they situate themselves in a particular context and as they consider greater contexts—audiences in writing, teachers of writing, other classrooms, college, etc. In *Literacy: Reading the word and the world* (1987. South Hadley, MA: Bergin & Harvey.), Paulo Freire states that a teacher must appreciate how individuals are engaged in negotiating their ways through conflicts imposed by various social contexts. Such an appreciation, Freire contends, is critical to an education in which students can become conscious of the conflicts, and thereby have some control over how they would negotiate their ways through those conflicts. Freire puts it this way:

> I believe that a critical education, an education along the lines of what Henry Giroux calls radical pedagogy, has to consider this tension and has to understand how this tension between the individual and the social practice takes place. . . . When challenged by a critical educator, students begin to understand that the more profound dimension of their freedom lies exactly in the recognition of constraints that can be overcome. Then they discover for themselves in the process of becoming more and more critical that it is impossible to deny the constitutive power of their consciousness in the social practice in which they participate. On the other hand, they perceive that through their consciousness, even when they are not makers of their social reality, they transcend the constituting reality and question it. This behavioral difference leads one to become more and more critical; that is, students assume a critical posture to the extent that they comprehend how and what constitutes the consciousness of the world. (47–49)

After reading Brooke and Hendricks we might be better equipped to assist students in becoming conscious of the social factors that affect their growing senses of identity. Brooke and Hendricks' study provide us with a framework with which to appreciate the kinds of conflicts students confront. They remind us that we are never really initiating students into our academic culture. Robert Brooke was the one entering our academic-discourse community. His students, on the other hand, were entering a community akin to our own but nevertheless different. One difference, we are told, would be in how we regard learning. We consider questions of audience as ends in themselves, for example. We are concerned with learning more about the nature and dynamics of discourse, because we find these dynamics inherently interesting. We are concerned—as is this study—with our abilities at teaching these dynamics, because we believe others should recognize the importance of consciously constructed discourse. We are, whatever our insecurities in the classroom and elsewhere, generally comfortable with our senses of selves as members of the communities of teachers, researchers, scholars. For most of our first year students, however, learning is a means to something else: an as yet not clearly defined sense of identity. They are developing their senses of selves, with our classes as critical factors in that development. We must appreciate our contextual roles in that development without giving in to the paternalism those roles can invite. This is a difficult constraint on us as well as the students, a conflict *we* must negotiate. The following pages will prompt us to consider some of the ways we inadvertently pose conflicts for the students we would help, and how students negotiate their ways through and around those conflicts. The study will provide us with yet another way to be critical of our own practice.

Introduction

THIS STUDY ADDRESSES A PEDAGOGICAL PROBLEM: HOW CAN WE teach "writing for an audience" in an institutional setting where students know that the teacher, not the addressed audience, assigns the grade? Won't students spend far more time trying to figure out what teachers want than they will considering how they might write to actual audiences? This is a crucial problem in contemporary writing instruction.

In the last decade, many researchers and teachers have identified the importance of considering a writer's audience. Flower et al. (1986) and Sommers (1980) have argued that one of the significant differences between beginning and experienced writers is the ability to represent a rhetorical task effectively, and a central aspect of task representation is effective portrayal of audience. Lisa Ede's work with the theory of audience (1984; Ede and Lunsford 1984) suggested that effective writing always involves a complex interplay between meeting the demands of readers and creating within the text a workable stance for readers to take—an interplay that much writing instruction is presently unable to address. Patricia Bizzell (1982) has argued that a writer's task is largely defined by the discourse community in which she writes and that the greatest task facing writing teachers and researchers is to help students understand the social conventions and practices that constitute the discourse communities they wish to enter. All of these scholars suggest that a writer's audience—the community of readers who will use the texts the writer produces—is an important and central influence on writing, and that helping students understand the full complexity of "writing for an audience" should be an important goal in writing instruction.

The pedagogical problem is how to translate this insight from theory and research into student experience. Students in writing classes, after all, are not really writing for the "discourse community" they wish to enter. They are not actually writing, for example, for executives in corporations, for scholars in refereed journals, or for the readers and editors of literary magazines. Instead, they are writing in an instructional setting in which teachers will read their work, evaluate their writing and class participation, and assign grades based on their overall performance. Is "writing for teachers," even when teachers explicitly assign students to pretend to write for other audiences, in any significant way the same as "writing to an audience"? Peter Elbow (1981) has captured the essence of this problem by comparing writing for teachers to playing tennis for a coach. Writing for teachers, he explains, is like hitting a ball against a wall while your coach is watching; writing for an audience is like playing tennis against a real opponent. In the former case, the way one plays will be evaluated; in the latter, what matters is the actual result of the game.

Our study seeks to understand how students make sense of "writing to an audience" within the institutional setting of a first year college writing course. We studied this particular class in 1983, while teaching in the University of Minnesota composition program. One of us (Robert Brooke) had designed a first year course that attempted, in the confines of the Minnesota process-based curriculum, to lead students to a fuller conception of audience. We were interested in this course both practically and theoretically. Consequently, we decided to study the course using a version of participant-observation methodology (described in detail in chapter 1). During fall quarter of 1983, the participant-observer (John Hendricks) attended all meetings of the class and several meetings of two small conference groups. He conducted taped interviews late in the quarter, one with each of two small groups, and one with the whole class. Both of us— as teacher and observer—recorded observations of, and reactions to, the class in journals. Students were required to keep journals as part of their coursework. Shortly after the course was completed, we taped a long conversation about our initial reactions to what had happened. These tapes and journals became the primary data for understanding the course.

Through long-term participation in this particular class we attempted to come to grips with the potential "double message" writing in such a situation presents to students. We hoped that extended observations in the classroom would show us both how the participants came to understand "audience" as a concept and what kinds of dynamics led to the understanding each person developed. Consider, as an introduction to the kind of data we gathered, the following excerpts from interviews with participants in the class we studied:

Kris: Other teachers aren't going to want what Robert [the teacher] wants, so we should—
George: Well that's the whole thing! You, ah, kind of what's good about this class—he's different, so you got to figure out what he wants, so—
Kris: I know, but—
George: You'll be able to figure out what they want.
Kris: Yeah, but, other teachers—So what are we going to—what are we supposed to do, get you know totally so that we know what Robert wants, and then every paper we write it's going to be, oh my god, you're writing for Robert, you know, you're writing for what Robert wants. Then you get to another teacher, and you're going to be writing *that* way—if that's not what *they* want, you don't have—
(Excerpt from small group interview, December 1983: see appendix 1 for transcription conventions and complete transcript)

Observer: [What did you want from students' writing?]
Robert [*Teacher*]: Well, it's writing to match, achieve some kind of purpose outside the classroom. Um, writing that appears with, in a form and organization and content and style appropriate for the needs of a given reader out there. And of course there's a great deal of subjectivity involved in that, because *I'm* evaluating *their* product on the basis of *my* conception of what the needs of the reader are. So there is a kind of double-bind there, for the—for the students. I think it's recognized. I mean they are aware—some of them in a very, um, *antagonistic* way, that I would say "Because we got to give Robert what *he* wants, even though we're pretending to give these guys what they want, otherwise he gives an F for it." (Excerpt from instructor interview, December 1983)

These excerpts show that all participants (students and teacher) were aware of problems, of conflicting messages, involving "writing to an audience" within the confines of their first year writing class. The students describe the problem as one of generalizability—will the kinds of writing rewarded in this class also be rewarded in other classes? Will the ideas about writing presented here generalize into other settings? Is the kind of audience faced in this class anything like the audience to be faced in future classes? The teacher describes the problem as a "double-bind" facing the students, a problem of having to do one thing while pretending to do another. For him, this double-bind is partly a problem because it led to antagonism from some of the students.

As writing teachers, we need to help students come to understand "writing for an audience" if we are to help them become better writers. But, as teachers and students, we all interact in an institutional setting that may work against any direct application or understanding of this idea. This study is an attempt to describe the complexity of this problem for teachers of writing and to use this description to suggest potentially useful ways of thinking about the social dynamics of writing classrooms in general.

We developed our description of this problem by drawing on two lines of research. The first is theoretical and involves the investigation of social forces that come into contact (and conflict) when individuals interact in educational settings. The second is methodological and involves participant-observation (a research method derived from ethnography) as a way of coming to understand the experiences of people culturally different from the researcher. Both lines of research were used to help us understand the problem: the theoretical work helped us pose questions and interpret the data we gathered; the methodology helped us gather information that other research methods would not have allowed.

This text proceeds in the following way. First, we present some background on the theories and methods used. Second, we describe in detail the particular writing class we studied, focusing especially on the experiences of four representative students who worked together in a small group throughout the quarter. We finish by drawing conclusions and discussing implications of our study regarding the dynamics of writing instruction and learning in general.

Audience Expectations
and Teacher Demands

1

Theoretical and Methodological Background

Some Theory: Classrooms, Conflict, and Identity Negotiation

The focus of this study is on a particular problem—learning "to write to an audience" from within a classroom structure where a teacher, and not the audience, assigns grades. The problem, in short, is one of potentially conflicting demands: the student writer needs to determine *both* what her chosen audience will need *as well as* what her teacher expects her to do, and these two demands will not necessarily agree. Therefore, how any individual student comes to understand the general concept of "writing to an audience" will have a lot to do with how she negotiates her position as writer and student in relation to these conflicting demands.

A useful way of looking at this problem is to see it as an instance of a more general problem in human development. As people mature, they are generally confronted with multiple demands on their behavior, demands that often conflict. Individuals often experience, for example, pressure from their families, their employers, their peers, and their religious organizations to act in certain ways. Often, these groups demand different and conflicting actions, thus placing individuals in a position where they must negotiate resolutions to conflicting demands. Such negotiation is an ongoing feature of human life.

This way of looking at human experience might be called a "conflict" view because of its emphasis on the conflicting demands facing individuals, or it might be called a "negotiation" view because of its emphasis on the strategies by which individuals negotiate livable resolutions to conflicting demands. Both ideas, conflict and negotiation, are central to this way of describing human experience. Both have been applied, moreover, to the particular dynamics of educational settings and to the general dynamics of human development.

Several recent studies have investigated the ways in which American education places individuals in conflict (in composition theory, see especially Annas 1985; Bizzell 1988; Brooke 1987; and Rose 1985). Henry Giroux's "conflict and resistance theory" of education (1981, 1983; Aronowitz and Giroux 1985) has gone the farthest toward presenting the general shape of such a view of education. Drawing heavily on the work of Paulo Freire (1970, 1973), Giroux argues that education presents people with conflict in two dramatic ways: first, education in our culture is a general topic for conflict, given the variety of groups in our culture who want to influence the ways children are educated; second, any educational setting presents individuals with conflict because the groups individuals belong to require radically different stances toward education and its dynamics.

As an example of these two kinds of conflict, Giroux cites the position of minority groups toward education. At the "topic" level, these groups often find themselves confronted with conflicting ideas: that education currently is biased against minorities, and hence should be resisted; that education is the only way to raise the social position of minorities, and hence should be embraced; that education needs to be changed generally to correct social biases against minorities. Because of these conflicting ideas, any minority member—of any age—is likely to experience stress concerning her behavior toward education. Furthermore, what school officials view as acceptable classroom performance will often conflict with what community groups expect of the individual. Researchers as diverse as William Labov (1972), Shirley Heath (1983), and Paul Willis (1977) have shown that young minority students often face one set of demands for school performance from teachers, principals, and "good" students, and another set of demands from peer groups and older members of the minority community. Because of these conflicts, many minority students become discipline problems in the eyes of school officials—largely because their disruptive behavior allows them to maintain their standing in the out-of-school communities.

Consequently, Giroux claims that schools throughout our culture are sites of conflict and resistance, places where individuals come into contact with conflicting groups and conflicting demands. As a result, young people and teachers unceasingly engage in negotiation, trying to resolve these conflicting demands in ways that allow them to feel comfortable. Any individual will of necessity have to find ways of supporting some groups and resisting others in the school environment if she is ever to feel even remotely comfortable at school. Of course, neither the conflicts nor the negotiations may ever be fully conscious, for these problems are so deeply rooted in cultural experience as to seem almost a "given" in school experience.

When looked at from the perspective of Giroux's "conflict and resistance" theory, our study clearly concentrates on only one kind of conflict in writing classrooms, the conflict centered around the concept of audience and compliance with teachers. We expect that college students experience a variety of other conflicts in writing classrooms (for example, conflicts between greek and dormitory values, between athletes and scholars, between majors, between political conservatives and liberals, between the sexes, and so on). Some of these other conflicts undoubtedly influence the way students perceive the student-teacher relationship and the way they perceive the audience for their work. Even so, the issue of how to comply with a teacher's demands when that teacher assigns "writing to an audience" is itself a complex and conflicting problem. We see this study, therefore, as illuminating only one small part of the complex dynamics of writing classes. Giroux's "conflict and resistance" theory provides a way of placing the problem our study investigates within the wider dynamics of classroom interaction.

Giroux's overall emphasis is, of course, on ways teachers and education specialists might understand and change school interaction by making such "conflict and negotiation" explicit. But another emphasis is equally viable: an emphasis on the experience of the individuals growing up in the school community and the communities that surround school. Individual development, when looked at from this perspective, also is involved in the ongoing interaction of individuals and groups and the conflicting demands groups place upon individuals. The kind of person any individual will become is likely to be a function of how that individual negotiates her way through the complex set of conflicting demands various groups make upon her.

Such an emphasis on individual development through conflict and negotiation is the emphasis taken by a host of social psychologists. These theorists claim that human "identity" is the product of such conflict and negotiation, rather than being some hypothetical "core" element like a soul, an essence, or an individual spirit. These theorists are often called "identity theorists" because of their focus on how human identity is formed.

Our understanding of this position in social psychology comes most directly from the work of Goffman (1961, 1963, 1967), Erikson (1950, 1968), and Laing (1960, 1961, 1967, 1982; Laing and Esterson 1970), although the position is widely held. These theorists are all concerned with the ways an individual comes to experience herself as a valid part of, or as alienated from, her social environment. "Identity," in the sense that these theorists use the term, is a function of this interaction between individual and environment. It is not the same thing as the Romantic idea of the inviolate quality at the core of the self; instead, "identity" for these theorists is a social construct, a product of social interaction.

In fact, "identity" is in many ways a misnomer for the concept these theorists have in mind, for the word "identity" implies something single, unified, and whole, while these theorists have something fragmented and dynamic in mind. In a way, these theorists present human identity in much the same way as portraiture is presented in a work like Duchamp's *Nude Descending a Staircase*. Instead of portraying a person in a single, static snapshot (thereby fixing the person at one point in time), Duchamp's painting shows the dynamic motion of a body descending the stairs. Single features cannot be made out, but a sense of the body's movement and dynamism is conveyed. "Identity" for theorists like Goffman, Erikson, and Laing is a lot like the dynamic body in Duchamp's painting. Rather than focusing on any individual's sense of identity at any single time, these theorists are primarily interested in the ongoing dynamics through which a person's sense of identity appears: the dynamic interaction between individual and social environment.

In fact, for these theorists the development of human identity basically involves an ongoing interaction between social and internal definitions of the self. The dynamics of identity take place in the distance between the identity "implied" by a person's behavior in any given social environment and the identity "felt" by a person as most truly hers.

This distinction between an identity implied by social interaction and an identity an individual "feels herself to be" is derived from identity theorists' distinctions between various meanings of the term "identity." Looking at these distinctions is useful in making sense of the experience of students in writing classrooms, for they allow us a vocabulary for describing some of the tensions they face.

For these purposes, the distinctions presented by Erving Goffman's *Stigma* are helpful. In *Stigma*, Goffman distinguishes three meanings of the word "identity," each of which relates to social interaction and individual experience in particular ways. The first two meanings explain "implied" identity, the last meaning explains "felt" identity.

First, for Goffman, the term "identity" often refers to a person's "social identity"—that is, the classifications of an individual others will make based on first impressions. Clothes, bearing, accent, physical attractiveness, cleanliness, and the like all come into play here. The student in the class we studied who often wore his Navy uniform was using this aspect of identity to be seen as a certain kind of person. Obviously, different social contexts assign an individual different social identities based on the same appearances. In this class, the uniformed student stood out because he was the only one in uniform; in his military history class, however, he would have seemed just like everyone else. In any context, then, how a person immediately appears carries with it implications about identity, and different contexts value different appearances.

Second, Goffman identifies "personal identity" as a meaning of the term "identity." Goffman defines "personal identity" as the sum total of physical or biographical information known or attributed to an individual in a given context. Unique physical attributes—a facial deformity, for example, or great beauty—are marks of personal as well as social identity, but more important for this category are the biographical records left by an individual's journey through life. These records take two forms: the official paper trail of birth certificates, school attendance, wedding licenses, and the like; and the informal memories other people have of the individual. Different contexts value different aspects of a person's past, of a person's personal identity, just as they value different aspects of social identity. In their initial self-descriptions for the class we studied, for example, students were asked to write about past writing experiences, a favorite writing class, and their writing processes, because these were the aspects of their personal history most important to a writing class. Other aspects (police record, marital status, etc.) are not as important in this context, although they may be in others.

Taken together, these two aspects of "identity" define the sort of "identity" a context is likely to assign an individual. Each social context will value certain kinds of immediate appearance (social identity) and certain information about an individual's past (personal identity). Different contexts value different things. In college writing classrooms, one's appearance (social identity) is open to a wide range of variation—as long as one is clean, odorless, quiet, and dressed one can be a viable participant in college classes. But personal identity is another matter. As the course progresses, individuals' "paper trails" of work, papers, and grades begin to assign identities to the participants. As a consequence of these paper trails, some individuals become successful students, others marginal students, others average students. The teacher's recollection of how individuals behave in class, what they contribute, and the success of their reasoning likewise contributes to this classification of students. As the course progresses, then, these features of the interaction begin to "imply" an identity for each individual within the classroom context.

Goffman's third meaning for "identity" leads beyond the identities that situations imply to the identities people feel themselves to have. An individual's alignments toward the groups that surround her define what Goffman calls "ego identity" (in Erikson's sense of the person's guiding self-conception). Individuals will, Goffman points out, be perceived as "a member" of some groups and as "an outsider" in others, largely as a consequence of their social and personal identities in various situations. How persons align themselves to these groups lets others know a great deal about the self they wish to be or project. The student who wore his Navy uniform to class on more days than was required, for example, did so to assert his membership in the military as a positive and forceful aspect of his identity. Other R.O.T.C. students project different alignments to the military by such behaviors as only wearing uniforms when they have to, by arguing against U.S. foreign policy when the subject comes up, or by painting peace symbols or philosophic statements on their military apparel (like the soldier in Kubrick's *Full Metal Jacket*). By these behaviors, individuals show their alignments to the groups they seemingly belong to. The particular ways individuals align themselves to such groups thus shows a great deal about how they conceive of themselves. It gives us a window, as it were, on their felt identity.

In fact (though Goffman does not make this point), it is this sense of ego identity formed through group affiliation that largely guides the choices individuals make about how to present their social and personal identities. How a person chooses to appear and behave (social identity) is a consequence of what sort of person she wants to be classified as (the navy uniform, for example, classifies the wearer as a member of the military, and others will consequently make corresponding assumptions about this person's politics, worldview, and attitudes toward gender roles). Similarly, what a person chooses to tell about herself (personal identity) is influenced by how she wants others to understand her relationships to the groups surrounding her (one student, for example, wrote in her initial self-description that she wanted to obtain a Ph.D. in child psychology, thereby marking herself as a member of the college community).

A person's ego identity, understood as the particular set of alignments one holds to the groups one belongs to, thus guides the other versions of identity Goffman describes. The development and maintenance of an ego identity is, therefore, the central issue in identity negotiation. For an individual, the central problems are: What groups do I want to belong to? What groups do others think I belong to? How can I influence others (and myself) to believe I am a member of the groups I want to be in and am outside the groups I only appear to be in? Or are the others right, and I am actually not a member of the groups I aspire to and only a member of the groups I reject?

Such questions (in some form or another, conscious or unconscious) guide self-perception and behavior, for the ways an individual answers them provide motivation for public behavior and most of the tensions of private worry. An individual's psychic life, thus, can be thought of as endlessly concerned with her social place and the negotiation of group affiliation, for from her patterns of affiliations and rejection the individual arrives at her sense of self.

This process, of course, is not necessarily conscious, and is fraught with difficulty. In fact, it was the problems with this process that first led therapists like Erik Erikson and R.D. Laing to investigate identity as social negotiation. In dealing with disturbed individuals, it was often an extreme confusion about the person's social place or an extreme ambivalence about group affiliation that was at the root of the problem. This insight led Erikson (1950) to his famous concept of the "identity crisis" in adolescence, and Laing and Esterson (1970) to the investigation of how family interaction helped drive patients mad. In both cases, problems with identity negotiation were at issue. For Erikson's adolescents it was the confusing plethora of possible groups they could be members of (coupled with a sense of no longer "belonging" fully to their families) that caused the crisis. For Laing's schizophrenics, it was the plural and contradictory messages about affiliation that families sent the patients that led to their madness—within the family, the patient could not ascertain finally who she was allied with and who she was pitted against.

A person's group affiliation and ego identity, thus, are deeply related to health and sanity. If a person is unable to negotiate the different personal and social identities she is assigned and is unable to mold a particular pattern of group affiliation into an ego identity, then the person may be headed for madness, for a profound and unmanageable sense of disintegration (as studied in Laing's *The Divided Self*). On the other hand, if a person can negotiate a pattern of group affiliation and rejection to call her own and make her "self," then the person may attain a sense of congruence and integrity.

Consequently, Erikson (1968) poses the problem of identity as an interplay between "mutuality" and "crisis," between feeling acknowledged and rewarded as the person one "is" (which means, of course, feeling accepted by the groups one belongs to and rejected by the groups one rejects) and feeling unsure of identity because of uncertainty about which definitions of self to listen to. In the experience of most people, these two poles are intertwined, being tenuously resolved but also providing ample opportunity for private worry. Given the nature of our culture, claims Erikson, most of us have only a tentative sense of mutuality, and in moments of personal or social challenge this sense often collapses into a threatening sense of crisis.

For theorists like Goffman, Erikson, and Laing, then, the central problems in human development involve the conflicts between implied and felt identity. Throughout life, a person will experience conflicts between the identities assigned by social groups surrounding her and the identities she feels or desires. The resultant problem of development involves the resolution of enough of these conflicts so that the individual can function productively in society. Erikson (1968) calls this problem "identity formation" and gives the most thorough, if baroque, definition of its process: "[I]dentity formation employs a process of simultaneous reflection and observation, a process . . . by which the individual judges himself in the light of what he perceives to be the way in which others judge him in comparison to themselves and a topology significant to them; while he judges their way of judging him in the light of how he perceives himself in comparison to them and to types that have become relevant to him." (22–23).

The process of identity formation is thus a social process involving a complex web of several sets of judgments and several sets of actions. Individuals develop a sense of self because of the ways they act, the ways others respond to those actions, and the ways they respond to those responses. There are, of course, many possible ways these judgments and actions can come out, given the number of social groups that might surround an individual and the multiple ways a person might respond to those groups. Some of these possibilities occur in school settings, and hence in education the social forces that theorists like Giroux analyze intersect with the processes of identity development analyzed by identity theorists.

Our study clearly investigates a kind of interaction that is deeply concerned with implied and felt identities. How an individual understands the teacher-student relationship and the notion of "audience" for her classroom writing obviously influences a number of implied and felt identities. A young person's role as "good, bad, or average student" is influenced by this relationship, as is a student's sense of how well she belongs to the group of college-educated people. For many young people, the issue of a college education and what it implies about themselves is a serious issue for identity development, clearly influencing who they will "feel themselves to be" in the future. Our focus on student experience of the conflicts between teacher demands and audience expectations in writing classrooms is clearly a focus on only a small part of these ongoing identity negotiations in the college years.

These two lines of thinking (conflict-and-resistance theory in education; identity theory in social psychology) both suggest that individuals experience conflict in social situations because of the multiple demands social groups place upon them. They also suggest that individuals work in many ways, consciously and unconsciously, to negotiate their positions in relation to these groups in ways that allow a productive sense of self to emerge. Schools, of course, are immensely important in these processes, because in schools many groups and individuals come together to interact in formative ways. The conflicts and negotiations that make up social resistance and individual identity are very active in school settings.

Such theories provide a useful way of looking at the problem this study addresses. When students have to negotiate between the different demands of teacher and chosen audiences, they are engaging in some of the same processes normally experienced in school and in identity formation. Some sort of negotiation between the conflicting demands of social groups will be involved. Any version of the general concept of "writing to an audience" a student produces will be influenced by the way that student handles these conflicting demands. Since these processes of negotiation and conflict are not entirely conscious, we would also expect that students' versions of their experience might take a number of different forms, some recognizing the conflicts they face, and some seemingly unaware of them.

Our study of one first year writing class relied heavily on these theoretical positions. We were interested in how students handled the conflicting demands "writing for an audience" presents. Conflict and negotiation theories of education (like Giroux's) suggested that we investigate the various ways classroom interaction influenced individuals as they worked to succeed in school. Identity formation theories (like those of Erikson, Goffman, and Laing) suggested that we investigate the ways individuals negotiated the distances between the identities implied for them in the classroom and the identities they felt or desired. We expected to find in the classroom we studied a way of describing the dynamics of teaching audience in an

American educational institution. These theoretical perspectives guided both the ways we investigated this problem and the ways we interpreted the data.

Methodology: Ethnography and Participant-Observation

To investigate the problem of "teaching writing for an audience" in first year classrooms, we used a version of the participant-observation methodology employed by Calkins (1983) and Heath (1983) in elementary schools, Kantor (1984) in high schools, and North (1986) and Brooke (1987, 1988) in college classes. In all these cases, researchers participated in classes for an entire school term, gathering as much data as possible about the class, the students, and the instructional setting. Then, after the course was over, the researchers worked to interpret or explain what they had found. This kind of research, often incorrectly called "ethnographic" because of its reliance on anthropological ethnographic principles, is based on a two-fold process of immersion into the "culture" of a classroom on the one hand, and careful reflection aimed at understanding that culture on the other.

The reasons for using participant-observation as a research method stem from the kinds of questions anthropological ethnographic researchers have traditionally asked. As Kantor et al. (1981) point out, educational researchers began to borrow these methods when they became concerned with the effect of context on learning and with students' perceptions of how education affects (or does not affect) their own experience. Since these topics involve qualitative issues of how people make sense of experience, quantitative or strictly empirical methods borrowed from the natural sciences were hard to employ usefully. Instead, researchers turned to anthropology, where questions about the context and perception of social experience had long been investigated.

Within anthropology, a long-standing tradition of ethnographic research exists. Because anthropologists have traditionally attempted to understand and describe cultures as members of those cultures experience them, anthropologists have studied cultures by living in them for extended periods of time, participating in and observing what goes on, and recording what native participants have to say. Shirley Brice Heath (1982) describes anthropological ethnography this way:

> The goal of ethnography is to describe the ways of living of a social group, a group in which there is an in-group recognition of individuals living and working together as a social unit. By becoming a participant in the social group, an ethnographer attempts to record and describe the overt, manifest, and explicit behaviors and values and tangible items of a culture. By long residence, the ethnographer learns the language of the society and structures and functions of cultural components, before attempting to recognize patterns of behavior that may be covert, ideal, or implicit to members of the culture. Ethnographers attempt to learn the conceptual framework of members of the society and to organize materials on the basis of boundaries understood by those being observed instead of using a predetermined system of categories established before the participant-observation. (34)

The goal of ethnography in anthropology, in other words, is to experience and understand the culture being studied as members of that culture experience and understand it—and this goal requires a slow, descriptive accumulation of information, categories, and ideas about the culture through the experience of living in it. All of the items that make up an anthropologist's field notes serve this end: all the maps, all the charts of kinship and interaction patterns, all the interviews, life histories, and descriptions of rituals and folklore are recorded in order to help the anthropologist come to see the culture as one living in it does.

Of course, the purely descriptive goal of "seeing the culture as those living in it see it" is only the first task of anthropological ethnographies, even though it is the most time consuming in terms of hours of research. Anthropologists also use their ethnographies as opportunities to reflect not only on the studied culture, but on their own as well—a chance to engage in a productive critique of what they learn. While anthropologists consistently warn against naive ethnocentrism in evaluating foreign cultures, part of the goal of their work is to be able to return to their own culture with insights drawn from afar, and as a consequence suggest improvements or new ways of thinking that might alleviate cultural problems.

It is this potential for cultural critique that makes ethnographies so important for many contemporary anthropologists. As Marcus and Fischer (1986) have argued, a carefully conducted ethnography allows the researcher two useful tools for critique: (1) data that show the varieties of experience within one particular culture, the varieties of ways in which people adapt to and resist the rules of the social order in which they live; (2) a vantage point *between* cultures, at the intersection of two cultures, from which to think about and evaluate cultural phenomena. As a consequence of such data and such a vantage point, an ethnographer can often articulate conflicts and problems in her own or her studied culture in ways that those living there can understand and use. Because she has a variety of accounts of experiences from *within* the studied culture, the anthropologist can articulate alternative and conflicting understandings of the same events in order to illuminate problems. Because she has knowledge of how *two* cultures handle significant problems in individuals' lives, she can speak to both cultures from *without*— from the perspective of an other.

> It is here that the power of ethnography as cultural criticism resides: since there are always multiple sides and multiple expressions of possibilities active in any situation, some accommodating, others resistant to dominant cultural trends or interpretations, ethnography as cultural criticism locates alternatives by unearthing these multiple possibilities as they exist in reality. (116)
>
> The task of ethnographic cultural critique is to discover the variety of modes of accommodation and resistance by individuals and groups to their shared social order. It is a strategy for discovering diversity in what appears to be an ever more homogenous world. The cultural critic becomes in effect a reader of cultural criticisms, discovered ethnographically, rather than an independent intellectual originator of critical insight. (133)

In short, within anthropology, ethnography has been used to understand how people foreign to oneself understand the social world and to articulate problems within the home and the studied societies in ways that can be experientially understood.

It is exactly these two uses of ethnography that have made its methods important for educational researchers. As Kantor et al. (1981, 294) point out, part of the impetus toward borrowing ethnographic methods in education stemmed from a feeling that research based on the quantitative natural science model was not producing needed changes in teaching. Researchers felt the need to describe how participants in classrooms actually experience learning and schooling in order to be able to prompt improvements in teaching. As in anthropology, the impetus toward importing ethnographic research methods in education involved the desire to understand and to critique, basing both the understanding and the critique of classroom practice on the information that comes from "living" in the classroom subculture.

Our study derives from this tradition of ethnographic research in anthropology and its use in education. We began with a sense of a problem in contemporary teaching—the problem of how students perceive audience within the institutional setting of writing classes. We sought to understand this problem by coming to see how students see it, from their experience in a college writing classroom. To this end, we sought to record both the ongoing daily activities of the class as well as the varieties of ways students reacted to and understood these activities.

Like most educational research that borrows ethnographic methods, our study is not a full ethnography. It is not an anthropologist's description of an entire culture. Our study is more limited in scope; it focuses only on student-teacher behavior in a single classroom, supplemented by out-of-class interviews and out-of-class student writing samples. We did not follow students or teacher into their private lives, nor did we attempt to describe other significant patterns of social interaction these people engaged in (e.g., dating, living arrangements, or daily work habits). Our study, however, did employ a dominant ethnographic research method—participant-observation—in order to address the pedagogical problem of "writing to an audience" in the institutional structure of a college writing class.

In order to understand the institutional setting of the classroom and the ways it structured students' experience, we gathered two kinds of data. First, the observer kept "field notes" in which he described daily activities in class, trying to record both what the teacher was doing and what the students were doing in response. Second, at the end of the quarter we collected all students' work for the entire term—all their papers, drafts, class notes, plans for papers, exercises, and written comments on other students' papers. These data provided a record of what Heath calls the "overt, manifest, and explicit behaviors, values, and tangible items" that structured the classroom culture.

In order to understand the variety of ways participants reacted to and comprehended class activities, the observer conducted four, forty-five minute interviews at the end of the quarter. He interviewed the whole class (without the teacher), two small groups of students who had worked together during the quarter, and the teacher. These interviews allowed us some access to the variety of ways participants in the class experienced their interaction, and some access to the forms of accommodation and resistance to class activities that participants employed.

During the three years following the class, we slowly worked to interpret this wealth of conflicting material, looking for ways to understand how students had experienced the class and for ways to use this understanding to improve our own practice (as teachers and researchers) in educational settings. We were guided in this work by the theoretical perspectives described in the first part of this chapter. This report is the result of this long process of interpreting the various forms of data we collected.

2

The Course

Background: The Minnesota Writing Program

The course we studied emerged against the backdrop of the writing program at the University of Minnesota as it existed between 1980 and 1985. Since 1986, Minnesota has been engaged in significant program revision, and the developing program is now describably different. Undergraduates entering the University of Minnesota in the year of our study took at least two composition courses, a first year course aimed at enhancing their writing processes, and an advanced junior-senior level course aimed at refining their writing for their major discipline. The first year course was generic; students from all majors participated in it. The advanced courses were specialized for students with majors in the social sciences, the natural sciences, engineering, and business, among others.

The explicit purpose of the first year course (as modeled in the training seminars for new teaching assistants during these years) was to make students more aware of their writing processes. The focus of the course was thus aimed more at their "prewriting and rewriting" stages than at the quality of the final drafts. Using a syllabus derived from Young, Becker, and Pike (1970) and Lauer et al. (1981), the program invited students to explore their topics on paper using a variety of heuristic strategies, to discuss their explorations and drafts with small groups of other students guided by the instructor, and to rework and reexplore their drafts using a variety of revision and organization strategies. The student's final grade in the first year course was usually based significantly on his or her "notebook" (a sort of running journal, workbook, and rough draft recorder in which all exploration and revision takes place) and on his or her participation in small group conferences with fellow students and the instructor. In evaluating the notebook and conferences, instructors took into account the quantity of student work, the quality and complexity of developing ideas, and the students' ability to use various tools and strategies to overcome their particular writing problems.

Other possible elements of writing—research methods, forms for scholarly apparatus, and patterns of reasoning and argumentation— were left for the junior-senior level courses in specific disciplines. These advanced courses focused on discipline-appropriate writing and involved heuristics for employing the concepts of the discipline, the types of writing tasks members of the discipline engage in, and any particular editing concerns and apparatus the discipline normally used.

Course Design and Teacher Rationale

The course we studied was a version of Minnesota's process-oriented first year course, offered in the fall quarter of 1983. It departed from the first year syllabus described above only by focusing assignments on the concept of audience. As in the course modeled in the training seminar, students kept a journal or notebook in which they recorded all their prewriting through revision work, and a third of their grade was based on this notebook. Students also worked in small groups, and their comments on others' papers also determined a third of their grade. Students were required to revise two of their papers until they were "perfect" and submit them at the end of the quarter for the final third. All of this was in keeping with the Minnesota first year curriculum as it existed in 1983; the experimental parts of the course were the assignments that were given and the guidelines for evaluating them.

Students were directed to write to "real" audiences outside the classroom (their bosses, consumers, students, etc.) and to design their texts for these audiences' needs. In theory, the approach was similar to Ruth Mitchell's and Mary Taylor's suggestions in "The integrating perspective: An audience-response model for writing" (1979) and Linda Flower's *Problem-solving strategies for writing* (1985): the emphasis was on developing "effective" writing as de-

fined by the imagined responses of "real world" readers to whom
one wrote. The teacher's hypothesis was that the form and content
of effective writing varies according to the social context in which
one writes, and, if students could be brought to see how audiences
influence the type of writing that is acceptable, they would be more
likely to produce effective writing by considering the characteristics
and needs of their audiences. During an interview at the end of the
semester, the instructor explained this idea:

> Kind of the underlying assumption behind all this I guess is that the so-
> cial context defines the substantive questions which define the formal
> characteristics of a piece, and if you approach it through that inverse pyr-
> amid you'll get to the right kind of formal characteristics almost by induc-
> tion. (Excerpt from instructor interview, December 1983)

The concept underlying the course, in the teacher's mind at least,
involved the relationship between text and context. If students
could see that social context defines what questions readers will find
interesting, and that these questions in turn help determine the
structure of texts, then students should arrive at form "almost by
induction." One purpose of the course, thus, was to help students
arrive at an understanding of the relationship between text and context, so they could use their understanding of context to help shape
any text they had to write.

The instructor consequently designed this ten-week course to get
students to think about how audiences influenced texts and to write
to a variety of audiences. The course was designed in five, two-week
blocks. During the first week, an assignment would be given, a variety of tools would be presented which were intended to help with
the assignment, and students would write a draft of their paper. On
Monday of the second week, students turned in xeroxed copies of
their papers to the teacher and to a conference group of three or
four other students; classes on Wednesday and Friday were can-
celed, and instead each small group would meet for an hour with the
instructor to discuss the drafts. Students were encouraged to call
the instructor by his first name, Robert.

The writing assignments were sequenced as follows:

First Assignment: Students were told to write about the same
subject for two different audiences. Robert's example was writing
about tax law for a New York banker and a Minnesota hunter.

Second Assignment: Students were told to analyze the way language is used in a particular social situation by observing and describing a complex situation for language use in contemporary culture. To help students in their analysis, Robert presented Young, Becker, and Pike's tagmemic system (in which a subject is viewed both as static, dynamic, and part of a system, and as something that contrasts, varies, and is describably distributed). Robert's example was an analysis of how people behave during midnight screenings of the *Rocky Horror Picture Show.*

Third Assignment: Students were told to write about the same subject in three different forms, making sure each was appropriate for an audience. The forms suggested were an outline, an issue tree (Flower 1985), and a collage (Elbow 1981). Robert's example was a handout with three pieces on manic-depressive psychoses—an outline for a formal speech, an issue tree for a popular article, and a collage much like a short story.

Fourth Assignment: The last two assignments were aimed at what Robert called "academic audiences." Students were directed to think of a writing project that would be appropriate for a paper in one of their classes. For this assignment, they were told to write a proposal for their paper "as if they were writing it to the Independent Study Office to get credit for doing the paper." Robert's example was an independent study form. The fifth assignment was also given at this time so students could use the proposal as preparation for their fifth assignment.

Fifth Assignment: Students were directed to "write the paper they had proposed, appropriately for their intended audiences." Robert's examples involved samples of academic writing in different fields.

All these assignments explored different aspects of the text-context relationship. The sequence of assignments, however, was intended to lead students to a better understanding of college audiences by the time the course was over. In an interview, Robert explained the ideas behind this sequence:

> So the course is designed, uh, in two parts. The first part is kind of a debugging section—that's the first six weeks—which I attempt to get them to see how task and process, uh, differs, alters, changes, based on what they're doing, what they think, uh, what their audience is and—and what the writing is supposed to look like, and such as a consequence.

And once *that's* done, then we can *re-ask* them questions about writing for *college* audiences, and hopefully what we've done is to put into place some new eyes to see with—the problem adequately, um, so that when we say "write a, write a humanities paper or a paper for your psychology class" or something, they will be able to focus on the, the right sort of issues to be able to produce that kind of paper, rather than being bound by the formal things they were taught in high school.

(Excerpt from instructor interview, December 1983)

As the instructor saw the course, then, the first three assignments were intended to exemplify aspects of the audience-text relationship, and the last two assignments would allow students to apply their new understanding of this relationship to the kinds of academic tasks they would be facing in the next few years. The changes Robert expected to see in his students would be less in their writing than in how they thought about writing, and this new way of thinking would "pay off" on the final two assignments.

As designed, then, Robert's course had two aims. First, he wanted to "get students to see" a way of looking at the text-context relationship. This was a kind of developmental aim on Robert's part and involved assumptions that students did not already see writing this way and that they needed to be guided to this insight by a series of exercises (rather than, for example, by simply being told or asked about the relationship). Second, he wanted to help students "understand" how to write college papers, by which he meant helping them understand how different the demands of college were from the demands of high school. This aim also rested on several assumptions, including assumptions that high school teachers taught "only form," that college teachers want something different from "only" formal competence, and that what college teachers want is in some ways harder to figure out than what high school teachers want.

Your writing that gets by the comp teacher in high school, uh, is a qualitatively different thing from the writing that gets by, uh, most of the professors here at the university. There are certainly the things that would— that we grow to write, and older people, um—and in some ways it's a bit of a happening to *alert* them to that, especially when, um, because of the difference in task I think there is a difference in writing process. So that all that stuff we tried to ground as, as gospel, about writing, really doesn't

hold true unless we're talking about some of these more complex tasks.
(Excerpt from instructor interview, December 1983)

Robert's course, in short, was intended to develop students' thinking about writing and to help them understand academic writing. These intentions seem to be fairly common among college teachers. In Robert's case, they were clearly related to his own position in academia.

As a graduate student in the final years of a doctoral program, Robert was beginning to write for publication in his field of composition theory and was in the process of applying for academic positions. He was also in the midst of a dissertation that argued that students go through a process of "socialization" during the college years and that this process can be seen in changes in their writing. In each of these activities, he was both succeeding and failing. Some of his work was being encouraged for publication, but most of it wasn't. It was too early in the academic year for any colleges to be responding to application letters. Robert's dissertation readers were split between those who thought his work was very good and those who found it unorganized and incoherent. In short, Robert was an initiate of the academic community when he taught this class and was very concerned whether or not he would be able to become a full member of that community. These issues, in fact, came up in an indirect way during the interview, while Robert and the interviewer were discussing Robert's thoughts on "academic writing":

> *Robert:* The writing's got to come out with the answers to the problem in some way, couched well enough that they acknowledge the, all the other viewpoints. And they get their knowledge, and it's "how do I know it's true" type stuff. You've got to go through that, the relativist track, tie them all in, because otherwise it comes out like sermons, which isn't what you want—
> *Interviewer:* Mmm, I, it's sort of funny, but this is a *lot* of what I heard being said when people responded to your text, um, the other day at the colloquium. It wasn't that there was anything necessarily wrong with the text, but a lot of what I heard was "You can't do this, Robert. That's not how you play the game."
> *Robert:* Yeah.
> *Interviewer:* Lily was saying, and I thought about that a bit—

Robert: Well *Gordon* was, I'll tell you—
Interviewer: Yeah, Gordon was.
Robert: He said, "Make it look like an academic text, damn it!"
Interviewer: Yeah.
Robert: Yeah.
Interviewer: But I mean, the, the real, you know, the people who are members of your church were excited about that sort of thing. It was interesting to me to, to see the sort of disjunction between Don's response and Lily's response and, you know, the community isn't all that cut and dried anymore—
Robert: No, it isn't.
(Excerpt from instructor interview, December 1983)

In this excerpt, Robert and the interviewer began by talking about the features of academic writing Robert felt were important, but they moved quickly to discussing how Robert's own writing was being received by the composition specialists at Minnesota. Both were very aware that Robert's work was meeting with mixed response and that there was serious disagreement over whether his work was appropriate for academics in his field. Hence, for Robert, success at academic writing was clearly an important issue, since it was not obvious that he could succeed at it. Academic writing was the kind of writing that really counted, and understanding the academic context well enough to succeed in it was a vital issue in his life.

It is thus not surprising that Robert's course aimed at understanding academic writing nor that his course assumed he had ways of thinking about writing that students did not. Robert's position within academia was implicated by these aims and assumptions. Since he was committed to becoming an academic, he saw this writing course as the first step in a long process of initiation into academia, and hence focused on understanding college audiences. Since he was applying for jobs as a composition specialist, he was also committed to the idea that he knew more about writing than most other academics (and certainly more than most students), and thus designed his course around the knowledge he felt he had that others did not. Furthermore, since his position as an academic was not yet secure (the job search could go wrong), he needed to defend his own sense of membership in academia. Robert's course grew out of these experiences; it was, as he told the observer in a private interview, the kind of course he wished he had had at the beginning of his college career.

Classroom Interaction

Discussions during class and group conferences tended to focus on the relationships among text, context, and audience which Robert felt he was teaching. Class discussion during the first week of each assignment was spent using a variety of tools for audience analysis and a variety of tools for content development. Conference discussions during the second week of each assignment focused almost exclusively on how appropriate each draft was for its audience, whether it had more than one audience or no audience, and how it could become more audience-directed. Robert usually directed the discussion, though the students did most of the talking.

A typical class period was conducted as follows: Robert would enter the room before the bell and ask if there were "any questions left over from last time." Often, students would ask for the assignment to be clarified—just what sort of thing did he want? Could he give them an example? At the time, both teacher and observer interpreted most of these requests as questions about the form the writing should take. Robert would invariably respond by telling the students to "figure it out on the basis of audience," since he was interested in students' ability to produce appropriate form through consideration of audience needs. He would then give an example: "If you were writing for *this* kind of audience, then you would design *this* kind of form because they have *these* sorts of needs." Students rarely seemed satisfied with these examples, however, and frequently a good fifteen minutes would be spent working through them. Robert consistently refused to be more specific about the form he wanted for each piece, arguing that since each student's audience would be different, each student would have to design her text with consideration for a particular audience's needs.

After discussing the assignment, class would begin. Robert would explain how a tool for audience analysis or content development would help with this assignment and would model the use of this tool using a volunteer's topic. Topics covered ranged from freewriting, to issue trees, to Aristotelian audience analysis, to Young, Becker, and Pike's tagmemic matrix. The class usually became engrossed in these exercises, and the period would usually end while the class was still involved in the application of the tool to the volunteer's topic. Robert would then summarize the main points of application as the bell sounded. Following class, he would privately answer questions from four or five students (usually more requests for clarification of the assignment, or for how today's tool would apply to their topics).

During the second, or conference, week of each assignment, students would bring copies of their papers for conference groups on Monday, and Robert would meet separately with each group on Wednesday and Friday. In conferences, students discussed each paper in turn, having read them beforehand. Discussion usually focused on how well the paper would meet the needs of its audience, and ideas for revision were based on improving the audience's reaction, on narrowing the audience, or on finding an audience for the ideas. Students would leave conference groups to revise their work before turning it in again the next Monday—and the sequence of modeling tools in class, then meeting in small groups, would repeat.

Overall, Robert's course was dominated by the concept of an audience who would read, use, and evaluate one's prose. While a variety of tools aimed at invention, exploration, organization, and revision were taught, they were taught within a framework that focused on the need to satisfy an audience. The process tools were taught as a means to an end, rather than as an end in their own right (as they would be, for example, in a writing workshop of the sort described by John Rouse [1985]). Writing was linked to satisfying the audience in all aspects of classroom interaction—both in class discussions and in conference group meetings.

Student Writing and Teacher Response

Robert's evaluations of student papers focused on the appropriateness of the text for the intended audience. His written and spoken comments usually pointed out features and ideas in the writing that the audience would accept, and features that would confuse, annoy, or disappoint them. Robert gave two grades for each paper. One was a grade for "how well you got the point of this assignment"; the second represented what grade the paper would receive if turned in without revisions as one of the "perfect" papers at the end of the term. A typical grade was an A or B over a C. Robert required at least one revision of every paper and allowed as many revisions as the student desired for the two papers submitted at the end of the quarter. His responses, thus, were intended to prompt revision and reconsideration of how the student's writing might better meet the needs of her audience.

Typically, his written comments were less extensive than spoken comments in group conference meetings. He claimed to use the written comments as reminders for what to talk about in conferences, rather than as extensive responses in their own right. An example of a student text as it moved through Robert's course follows. The first draft was turned in for the second assignment. The final draft, after several revisions, became one of the student's final papers in the course. Stacy, the student who wrote the paper, was a member of one of the small groups we studied extensively. The text of her first draft follows:

Stacy H.

Comp 1011

Your First Classical Guitar

Buying a guitar is like buying a car—everyone has different reasons for choosing one brand over another. What may sound good to you may not sound good to your friend. But there are a few things that anyone should consider when buying a classical guitar.

If you are a student with a limited budget, do not allow a dealer to convince you to buy a guitar which is well out of your price range. A higher price tag does not always mean better quality. A good classical guitar need not be a brand name, just be built well and have good sound.

If you are a beginner, I suggest that you go for the very low-priced models. This sounds like a cheap idea but it's possible for someone who is first starting out to become disenchanted and quit after a few weeks. But if you have some experience with guitar playing and are convinced that this is a serious move, then go ahead and look at the more expensive models.

Since a beginner probably doesn't know just what to look for when buying a classical guitar—such as types of wood, action and intonation—it is best to bring a knowledgeable friend along when shopping for your guitar.

The wood of the classical guitar is important. Be certain that the sales-person tells you what the guitar is made of. The top, or soundboard, of a classical guitar should be made of a soft, porous wood such as spruce or pine while the sides and back should be made out of a harder wood. Rosewood tends to be considered the best, although mahogany and maple are also good for the back and sides. The reason for the different types of wood is so the sound will come out of the front rather than the back and sides.

Another important thing to look for, especially for a beginner, is the action. Action is the ease or difficulty with which the guitar plays. It often refers to the distance between the strings and the frets. High action means a greater distance than low action. When you first begin to play, your fingers tend to get sore if the strings are too high. This can disgust a person and cause him to choose to stop practicing.

Always choose a guitar that is comfortable for you to play and fits your body size. A small person should not run out and buy a Gibson Super 400 because they will barely be able to reach around it. While on the subject of size, keep in mind that a wide fingerboard could be troublesome. I have small hands and prefer the fingerboards which are narrower than most classicals but wider than the average steel-string acoustic guitar. It is a minor problem but it could make a difference.

Another important factor to remember is the intonation of the guitar. Intonation is how well it stays in tune when different chords are played. It takes a fairly experienced ear to recognize this so be sure to ask that friend of yours with the experience to help you or ask the salesperson to help you.

Take your time when purchasing your classical guitar and don't let the salespeople push you. Sit down in a quiet spot and try a few chords. Try out a large selection of types and styles. Ask your friend to play it as well so you can hear how it sounds to your listener. Plus, once you have de-cided on a particular model, try two or three of the same model. Two guitars can have different sounds even though they were made by the same manufacturer and have identical features.

Once again, be sure to bring along a friend who will know what to look for. Otherwise a salesperson could sucker you into believing that one model is better than another simply because it costs fifty dollars more. Also never buy a guitar just because it looks pretty and has lots of lovely inlay between the tuning keys.

When deciding to purchase a guitar, whether at a music store or from a private party, never neglect the chance to bargain. They are often eager to bargain if they feel that is the only way to get you to buy it. If you find that you can't decide between two guitars, I suggest that you choose the one with the longest warranty. Once you have decided on the guitar, never neglect to buy a sturdy case which fits your guitar well, especially if you do alot [*sic*] of traveling. Keeping these thoughts in mind, jump right into the challenge of finding the best sounding guitar to meet your needs and price range. Playing a classical guitar can be a very rewarding experience and I wish to you many years of enjoyment with your new investment.

Stacy's first draft shows the organizational features of what Linda Flower (1979) calls "writer-based" prose. The text is basically an extended list of ideas related to buying a guitar, put down in the order they occurred to the writer. Sometimes ideas are brought up in several different contexts (such as bringing a friend along), and sometimes the writer shifts ideas without warning (for example, the sudden introduction of "fancy inlays" and "warranties" in the tenth and eleventh paragraphs). The most frequent transitional devices are "also" and "another"—devices that move the text to the next item on the growing list of ideas relevant to buying guitars. In short, one gets the sense of a writer remembering and adding material as it occurs to her in the process of writing.

But, no matter how writer-based the organization, Stacy's text shows the beginnings of an awareness of an audience and its needs. The entire text is set up as an aid to beginning guitar players, and the information she includes would generally be useful to such people. She is aware that some terms ("action," "intonation") are technical terms that beginners might not know and spends time defining them. She is aware of potential differences in her audience and writes different advice to those who are just beginning and to those with some prior experience.

In short, Stacy's first draft shows a fairly successful, if writer-based, attempt to communicate her knowledge to beginning guitar players. She has a sense of what they need to know and what vocabulary they lack. Where she runs into problems is in figuring out how to present this information in an organized and easily usable form.

Robert's responses to this draft reinforced the sense of audience Stacy exhibited and prompted her to consider how to present the information so her audience could use it more easily. His written comments served to identify the strong and weak elements of her text, and his guided discussion in conference expanded on the range of possibilities she had to choose from in improving the paper.

Robert wrote two comments on the paper itself. In the margin next to the first paragraph, he wrote: "Clear audience and purpose—those who wish to buy guitars will read on. Fine." This comment recognized that Stacy had found an audience to address and had good reasons for writing to it. This supported a kind of success on Stacy's part.

At the end of the paper, he wrote a slightly longer comment and a grade: "A/C. I read it all the way through without feeling prodded to make comments, which is a good sign. I felt like I was getting bounced around, though—you jump from woods, to $, to warranties, etc., without it ever being quite clear why. A bit more organization would help. Overall, a fine beginning." This comment identified the major drawback to Stacy's first draft—the fact that it "jumped around" and needed further organization—and again supported what she had accomplished. The grade reinforced these two messages, the "A" for getting the point of the assignment (clear audience/purpose), the "C" because more needed to be done before the paper was finished.

In Stacy's small group conference, these comments were fleshed-out. Robert took an audience-centered approach to the problem of organization, focusing primarily on how to design the text to make it accessible to the people who needed to read it. He began by asking where she thought she could present the paper so that beginning guitar players could use it. Initially, she wasn't sure, and said in a guitar magazine, she guessed.

The group then talked about the likelihood of beginning guitarists reading guitar magazines and about other places (like the newspaper) where beginners would be more likely to read this information. During the discussion, Stacy explained that she worked in a music store over the summer and that most of the customers really did not know anything about guitars when they came in and wouldn't have known where to look for an article on how to buy guitars even if they wanted to. Robert then suggested that maybe some kind of text in the store would help these people—like a pamphlet they could take with them, or a fancy poster with lots of information on it. Jane, another group member, mentioned a big poster she had seen that presented all the basic chords and fingering for guitar, and how one of her friends learned to play guitar from it. Under Robert's direction, the group talked for a bit longer about the pamphlets salespeople give out on merchandise and the way they are organized to provide a lot of information in an easy-to-use fashion. Summing up the discussion, Robert suggested that Stacy try to design her guitar paper as something customers could use in her music store. The group then moved on to discuss another student's paper.

Robert's strategy, in short, was to get Stacy to think about organization by considering how her audience might use the paper. Once she realized that a standard essay was unlikely to be used by her audience, she began to experiment with other forms. In her notebook for the next week, she wrote a list of ideas for converting her text into a pamphlet:

> My classical guitar pamphlet (leaflet?)
>   needs pics or illust. (take photos?)
>   go to podium again and other stores
>
>   definition of terms w/ diagram
>   lots of color
>   something they would see sitting on counter at music shop.
>   unless I want to get others interested. But then where would they
>   see it?
> I think a pamphlet for those already planning on buying an instrument or
>   at least the musically inclined since it would be seen at a music shop.
> Keep the truthful honest ideas in.
> Need to get more basic.
>
> Make outline—like list on front (numbered & they can find numbers
>   which interest them)
> This way audience can quickly scan the 1st page to see if this interests
>   them
> Write in 3rd person rather than the 1st person of 1st draft?
> Size of paper 4 x 8—several creases—accordion-type folds.

Some of this information came directly from the conference—the ideas of pictures, color, and a diagram of a guitar had been suggested by Jane while discussing the poster she had seen. Robert had suggested a table of contents so customers could skim easily. But much of it came from her own sense of what customers need and what she needs to find out. She suggested doing some research (returning to the Podium, a local music store) and keeping the text "honest" since she is aware customers often feel pressured by salespeople and documents. She also began designing the pamphlet itself, worrying about size and how to fold it. In short, Stacy has begun to design a document that could be used by readers in an environment she knows, rather than writing a list of somewhat disconnected ideas about guitar buying, all nominally addressed to beginning guitar players.

Stacy's next draft was an unfinished attempt at such a pamphlet. She had written a table of contents and drawn a diagram of a guitar with parts labeled, but she wasn't comfortable with it. She thought doing a pamphlet would take too long, both for her to design and for her audience to read, and was instead excited about making a large poster with what she called the basic "how to buy a guitar" information on it which the music store could put up in the guitar room. She said customers usually looked at the posters in the store, and this would be the best way to relay the information. Robert accepted her reasoning, and Stacy later completed her poster as one of her final papers.

In responding to Stacy's writing, then, Robert took an audience-centered approach, dealing with her organizational problem by getting her to consider the needs of the audience. Most of the real guidance went on in group conference discussion, where the issues she needed to address were explored. His written comments tended to be reminders of these points, with grades to indicate relative success on the assignments and the relative quality of the paper. Through the written comments, students could identify the major strengths and weaknesses in their work; through conference interaction, students were given a model of how to cure these problems by considering the needs of their audiences.

Student-Teacher Relationships

As the development of Stacy's text shows, students in Robert's course were able to understand much of what he meant by "audience" and were able to write documents that significantly addressed the needs of their readers. Nevertheless, responding to the course became a frustrating problem for many of the students. Throughout the course, the observer's daily notes were filled with examples of student unrest and frustration. Before Robert would arrive, for example, students often talked to each other about "what he wanted" and about their current understanding of assignments—talk that often led to "would you clarify the assignment?" questions when Robert arrived. Students also talked about how different their class was from others, and often struggled to identify whether or not this course had any connection to the rest of their college experience. They also compared and complained about grades.

When we looked at the grades and comments students were getting and at the papers they were writing, it was not clear why they were so frustrated. As the course progressed, most students (like Stacy) were able to write papers (or pamphlets or posters) that Robert approved of, and that showed a relatively clear conception of the needs of the group they were addressing. Most students received grades of "A over C" on their first drafts and slowly raised the "C" grades as they revised. Student frustration, therefore, did not seem explainable in terms of confusion about course content or about the evaluations they were receiving.

The reason for this frustration was not immediately apparent as long as we thought about it in terms of the concept of audience or the assigning of grades. When we thought about it in terms of conflicts and negotiations in the classroom, however, reasons for this frustration became clear. This classroom was an extremely confusing place for negotiating a comfortable sense of self because the roles it provided were contorted and the social relationships between individuals (especially between teacher and students) kept shifting.

Any classroom assigns the same individual different roles, different "implied identities," based on the different groups that interact there. Stereotypically, compliance with the teacher's demands results in being assigned a "good student" role by the teacher, a "smart person" role by those students who also comply, and a "teacher's pet," "nerd," or "earhole" role by those students who resist compliance. At the same time, other aspects of a student's behavior—for example, a male student's ability to make occasional wisecracks that other students can hear but the teacher cannot—will help assign the individual a role in peer interaction (for example, a "bad ass" role by other males or perhaps a "cute guy" role from some females). Any classroom is filled with such diverse and competing ways of assigning roles to individuals, and any individual thus negotiates her own position within the classroom by acting in ways that show the stances she takes toward each of these roles.

Robert's classroom certainly had these diverse and competing demands. One student, for example, wore his Navy uniform to class frequently and made numerous wisecracks while Robert was writing on the board. Some students laughed at his antics, and others acted disgusted by them. Such behaviors were used by all involved as "underlife" behaviors always are—to show there are other ways of understanding these people, other aspects to their selves, than the official interactions of the classroom can allow (Brooke 1987).

But Robert's course also produced a different sort of tension, one centered around "teacher" and "student" roles. Because of the multiple activities and responses Robert set up, students had to work through several different ways of understanding the teacher-student relationship, all of which operated at the same time. Since Robert's behavior as teacher supported each of these different ways of seeing the relationship, students found themselves unsure how to understand what the real expectations were for their behavior as students and, thus, were unsure how to negotiate the kinds of implied identities they wished to be assigned.

Robert's course produced at least the following three ways of understanding the teacher-student relationship, each of which provided different ways of negotiating an individual's implied identity as student:

1. "We're all writers, helping each other." Part of Robert's course supported understanding the class as a place where writers with different purposes and audiences met to share what they were working on and to help each other with these tasks. The conference group meetings, the acceptance of nonacademic texts like posters and pamphlets, and the use of student volunteers' real topics for class exploration all supported this understanding of the course. This way of seeing the student-teacher relationship, however, required that students define themselves in relation to a "self-sponsored writer" role—good students would be those who acted as self-sponsored

writers, working on and developing writings beyond the classroom; bad or marginal students would likewise be defined through the ways they did not exhibit these behaviors.

2. "Teacher is evaluator, student is performer." Another part of Robert's course suggested that teacher and student were operating within a traditional classroom structure where teachers give assignments, students do them, and teachers evaluate how well they did them according to some criteria, explicit or inexplicit. Much of Robert's behavior fit into this relationship. He assigned fairly specific writing tasks for students, he required all classroom tools to be tried at least once in the notebooks, he graded each draft of students' papers, and he did not write assignments along with the students (thus highlighting his position as evaluator instead of participant). All of these behaviors define the teacher-student relationship as that which is found in a traditional classroom, where explicit compliance with teacher demands is what assigns implied identities of good, bad, and marginal students.

3. "Diagnostician to developing adolescent." A third aspect of Robert's course was a relationship between teacher and student very much like that between a diagnostician and a developing adolescent. Robert gave two grades on each paper, one of which was for "how well you got the point of the assignment." He guided discussions in small groups to ways of thinking about audience and texts students might not bring up on their own. He emphasized the notebook, the "process," as much if not more than the "product," because he was interested in "how the notebook showed the progress of your thinking." Finally, he structured the assignments in the course as a progression of "exercises leading to a better understanding of audience." All of these aspects of his behavior suggested that he, as an older and more educated adult, knew things about thinking and mental development that the students did not and that he was diagnosing the course of their individual mental development as the quarter progressed. Such a relationship suggests a clinical or psychiatric relationship between teacher and student, in which students (like patients) would be defined as good or bad based on how well they responded to treatment.

Robert's behavior supported all three of these ways of seeing the teacher-student relationship. He maintained a helpful, supportive stance (like that demanded by the "we're all writers" version of the relationship). But he also maintained his position as an authority with whom students had better comply or face low grades ("teacher as evaluator") and as an authority who had a clear sense of how students' work was supposed to be developing as the course progressed ("teacher as diagnostician"). No particular relationship was ever dominant in his behavior.

Student responses—especially their frustrations—can be understood in relation to the complex nature of the teacher-student relationship in this class. Each student somehow had to come to grips with Robert and what he was teaching, and this meant negotiating an understanding of what he was up to from the conflicting relationships the class set up. Robert's course, in other words, confronted students with a problem for identity negotiation in the classroom: how they were to understand themselves and their behavior depended on how they understood the "expectations" operating in this class, but the expectations were unclear because the teacher-student relationship was a mess of multiple and competing possibilities.

This conflict, of course, was only one conflict facing students in the classroom. Other conflicts abounded: greeks versus dormies, military versus liberals, conflicts over dating and sex roles, etc. This particular conflict was extremely important, though, because at issue for students was the sort of student they were expected to be. How they understood this expectation would influence in some ways how they understood their membership in the "community of college students" and their potential for success in college. These issues are tremendously important in a first year class because many first year students are trying to decide whether they belong in college at all or whether they should try some other line of work temporarily or permanently. The conflict over the teacher-student relationship, thus, was particularly dominant in this class because it related to the issue of membership in the college community in ways that other conflicts in the classroom did not.

The next section will present several representative student responses to this course. These responses show the power and complexity of conflict and negotiation as processes in classrooms, for each student had to find a way of resolving the tensions of Robert's classroom in ways that supported the sort of self she felt herself to be. The nature of each student's learning is largely a product of this process, for the way they understood what they learned is related to the sense of self they were able to work out amid the possibilities the course offered.

General Student Response

The students' responses to Robert's course were varied and dissonant. Throughout the course, the students seemed challenged and frustrated—they put in a great deal of work on each assignment, quizzed Robert about "what they were supposed to do," and became frustrated with his "figure it out on the basis of audience" answers. They discussed their understanding of assignments with each other before and after class and spent a great deal of time teaching each other outside of class what they had figured out. In our opinion, the average student in Robert's class put in a greater than average amount of work, primarily because of the effort required to clarify her sense of the class. On any given day, a student was likely to be uncertain whether she hated or liked the course—the students felt off-balance, not quite sure what was going on, but not quite out of control either.

This sense of being off-balance was reflected most strongly in the anonymous written responses we asked for during the final class period. Of the twenty (of twenty-two possible) responses we received, three attacked the course, two praised it, and fifteen gave uneven responses, praising some things and condemning others. The content of these responses, though, was more uniform than their sense of the course. All twenty responses mentioned some concern about grades and the criteria for evaluation—the class as a whole felt very uncertain about how evaluation took place. For the three students who attacked the course, it was this uncertainty about evaluation that they disliked most intensely. On the other hand, seventeen of the twenty students felt they learned a lot about audience analysis and about how important audience is for writing. Almost universally, they felt audience was something highly important that they had not been presented with before. The two students who praised the course based their opinion on the usefulness of audience. What was odd about the class's response, in sum, was the dissonance the students clearly felt. They felt unsure about their upcoming grades but also felt as if they had learned something important.

The overall sense of frustration and learning is perhaps best exemplified by the following student's written response:

> I don't think that the class was as bad as it seemed. I mean I was really frustrated during the quarter and lost but come to think of it I did change and learn some things about my writing which did help. The audience analysis was the most helpful for me. Conferences were good they basically kept me from dropping the course when I got discouraged. I found it to be a hard class in the aspect of trying to figure out what exactly I was supposed to do for my grade. I did learn things even more when I stayed after class and drilled Robert with question [sic] to see if I was doing the assignment right or not. I really don't know right now what my overall impression was because I am concerned about the grade I will get—I'm satisfied now but if the grade isnt [sic] too hot I may want to write the Comp department a nasty letter. I did learn to change my writing perspective to somewhat more of a college level writting [sic] rather than a high school level writting [sic]. This aspect of the class was very effective. I still stress that the assignments be made more clear in what is supposed to be done in each of the separate assignments.
>
> (Unedited anonymous student response, December 1983)

The major elements of all the students' responses—uncertainty and worry about grades, and a sense that they learned something—are reflected in this written comment.

The students' sense of uncertainty about the class was compounded because they knew this class was different from other first year composition classes. Many of the students lived in large dormitories with other first year students, and discussions with students in other composition sections identified this class as being unique. The discrepancy between this section and other sections of the course was one of the topics the students voluntarily brought up during a full class interview the observer conducted in Robert's absence on the last day of the quarter.

Jeremy: Well basically the whole comp department has a poor system of grading because it's all dependent on the teacher's, um—

Allen: Point of view.

Jeremy: point of view. Um—

Allen: I mean—Your writing could be good for one teacher, for another teacher could be terrible. Just up to the instructor you have. And so I mean, basically—you have to shape your writing to fit the instructor, no matter if your writing's good or not.

Laura: I think that—least from talking to other people who live on my floor and my friends—there doesn't seem to be any *unity* in the comp department. One friend of mine got *totally* different, not done any of the things we've done. She writes on all personal subjects that they, that are her own, nothing that she ever had to really think about. Another friend of mine, totally different on the other, you know, from both of ours.

(Excerpt from full class interview, appendix 2)

For some students, then, one of the significant elements of the course was its uniqueness. They realized it was unique because of the differences in teacher expectations throughout the composition program—differences they knew existed because of their discussions with other students. The students sensed that this uniqueness was potentially a problem and questioned whether this class would help them succeed in their later work. Robert could be a completely idiosyncratic teacher, unlike any other teacher they would ever have, or he could be "right" about audience and how to write. If the former, then the students would have wasted their time with a real loser; if the latter, then they would be ahead of their peers. At stake, in short, was how well this class prepared them for membership in the group of successful college people. It might have helped them become more like successful college people, thereby bringing them into membership in the academic community faster than their peers. Or it might have been unlike what other college people really do, thus keeping them further away from membership. Behind the class's discussion of the range of classes in the composition program, thus, lurked the wider and more important problem of their "belonging" in college. How they came to understand how Robert's class generalized, thus, was a significant problem, and was the source of serious divisions among the students.

Several of the students came to view Robert's ideas as right and found the class very useful, while others thought Robert to be idiosyncratic and, hence, saw the class as a waste of time. Jane, one of the students we observed in small group conferences throughout the quarter, found Robert's emphasis on audience helpful. Jane contrasted the focus on audience with her high school experience and decided that writing to an audience was both more helpful and more fun:

> It was mostly audience, this way—it do me a lot of good, 'cause, you know, I sort of said I never bothered figuring out who I was writing for, I just wrote the paper and handed it in, and the teachers didn't *care*. You, and, uh, and he had us write different *things*, so we *had* to write to different audiences. I think that helped.
> (Excerpt from small group interview, December 1983)

In contrast, Susan, one of the members of a second small group, was convinced that Robert's approach was idiosyncratic and dictatorial:

> I think *audience* is going to be *obvious*, I mean if you're writing a, um, the only person that has to read it really is your pro*fess*or, I mean that—it's *obvious*. That you're writing it to him. I don't know why he spent so much time on audience.
> (Excerpt from small group interview, appendix 1)

Robert as a "weird" teacher who teaches stuff that's more helpful than normal writing teachers, versus Robert as a "weird" teacher who unreasonably wants you to write his weird way—this was the choice the students found themselves having to make concerning their experience in this class. This choice was necessitated because of the stress the course caused. Students were uncertain about their grades, how good their writing was, how typical Robert was, and whether or not their experience would generalize. Overall, it was unclear what implied identities the course offered students. This meant that each student had to work out the conflicting possibilities for herself, and somehow had to determine what these possibilities meant for her position in college. The uniqueness of the course, in short, put a great deal of stress on their felt identities, on their senses of themselves as students, writers, and learners. How they chose to view the class was intimately connected with how they wanted to view themselves. As we shall see, those who embraced the course did so because it allowed them to feel more secure as students and writers; those who rejected the course did so for much the same reasons. The ambivalence most students felt about the course reflected in many ways the complexity of their experience, a complexity that made them unable to resolve conflicting notions of the course and their implied identities within it.

The Experience of One Small Group

In Robert's class, four or five students worked together throughout the quarter in conference groups. These groups read and commented on each other's writings, met together with Robert apart from the rest of the class, and frequently worked with each other outside of class. The observer took part in two of these small groups throughout the quarter. To clarify the nature of student response to Robert's course, we will discuss in detail the experience of one of these groups.

The most representative group we studied was comprised of four students, two female (Susan and Kris) and two male (George and Doug). These students interacted well throughout the quarter but varied tremendously in their responses to the course and their strategies for dealing with its demands. In our opinion, all four dealt successfully with the course, if we view it from their perspective, and all four had responses to the course that were representative of other students. The stances they took toward the course show the various ways students understood their experience and negotiated a position for themselves as students and writers in relation to this experience. A description of each student's experience in the course follows.

Doug

By traditional standards, Doug was the least successful student in this group. At mid-term, Doug was failing the class, but he managed to pull a "D" by the end. Doug, however, did not resent or dislike his position as marginal student—he was always pleasant to Robert and the other students and basically claimed to understand the class. By his own admission, Doug was not very interested in writing. In the first week of the quarter, he evaluated his typical writing process partly as follows: "How I feel about writing in general, is that I dislike it. That is not to say that I don't always dislike it, but seventy-five percent of the time, I don't look forward to it" (student journal entry).

Doug went on to say that he usually wrote a five-page paper in about three hours, claiming "in that time I should be able to say all the things I want to, but sometimes quality is lacking." He listed invention problems ("I need questions to ask that I can't think of myself, to ask") and procrastination as his biggest writing problems.

Throughout the course, Doug wrote comparatively short papers, averaging one or two pages when other students wrote five to ten. He claimed to sit and think a lot, though his notebook/journal remained relatively empty. When he turned in his journal on the last day, he had the following note attached to it:

Robert,

I didn't finish my last two drafts because I don't think it would make any difference in my final grade. I guess that is a terrible attitude to have, but I just can't shake it. Everytime I sit down to write tagmemics and audience analysis I draw a blank, and the only way I can finish the assignment is by just doing a draft. Taking the class over again will probably be the best thing for me to do since my GPA will be dragged down the tubes if I let it stand as is. I'm sorry if this disappoints you, but I guess Comp isn't my bag.

Sincerely, Doug.

During a taped interview with this group late in the quarter, Doug admitted he was only in the course because it was a requirement, and that, although he felt he understood what Robert was trying to do, he found the assignments vague:

Doug: I *understood* what he was trying to *do*, but I thought it was a little *vague*, uh—
Interviewer: How so?
[2 second pause]
Doug: Like it wasn't *explained* very well. It, I mean, like examples were given, and that was it, you were supposed to take it from there and know how to do it, you know.

George: And, well—
Doug: I couldn't—I couldn't really, I *understood* it, but I couldn't do it my*self* because . . . I just never could solve that, you know—
(Excerpt from small group interview, appendix 1)

This response was typical of a great many students: they thought they saw what Robert meant when he worked through examples in class but found themselves confused and frustrated when they tried to work on their own papers at home. In Doug's case, the gap between what he understood in the classroom and what he did at home was significant. The time required to overcome his confusion at home was more than he wanted to put in. Doug later explained that he thought Robert's course was less a normal first year composition course than a course "for people who wanted a writing career." This didn't particularly bother him, he said, it "just wasn't his thing." Doug, thus, separated himself from the course, claiming that both his and Robert's ideas were valid, but different: this was a course for writers; he had no intention of being a writer; therefore, his poor standing in the class was not a problem.

As a consequence of this stance, Doug supported his fellow student George's positive evaluation of Robert's ideas when Robert was attacked as a "weird" teacher by the two women in his conference group:

Doug: I don't think it's *his* way as much as it's the way it should be done.
[*Interviewer:* What do you mean by that, Doug?]
Doug: I mean that it's *not* his personal view, it's how he thinks, it's how he *interprets,* what the right way of writing *should* be done, instead of, it's *not* something that it's his *personal* view—
(Excerpt from small group interview, appendix 1)

He was able to like the course even though he was failing because he separated his felt identity from the implied identity he believed the course offered. Since he never intended to be a writer, it didn't matter that he was doing poorly. He could thus say both that Robert's ideas were fine for writers and that composition wasn't his bag. In Doug's mind, Robert's goals and his own goals were both valid, just different.

Doug found a way of understanding his relationship with Robert and the course that made his lack of success in the classroom acceptable. His version of Robert was a teacher who was an authority on writing who could be trusted if one wanted to be a writer (which he didn't). Doug accepted, in short, Robert's relationship to students as "a fellow writer" and "diagnostician"—he acknowledged that Robert knew more than students did about "how writing should be done" and that Robert really intended to help students write more effectively.

Interestingly, though, Doug came to this understanding precisely because it was easy to reject. Robert was teaching writers; Doug did not want to be a writer; therefore, his poor performance didn't matter. He placed himself outside the groups Robert's course sponsored. He saw the game Robert was playing and chose not to take part. The fact that he was failing did not mean he was a bad student or Robert a mean teacher—it merely meant they differed over how valuable "being a writer" was. As Doug's note at the end of his notebook showed, he wanted to leave this class "agreeing to differ" with Robert. He would find his way into another class next quarter—where, apparently, a different relationship between Doug and his teacher would be in effect, and where he might succeed because "becoming a writer" would not be the goal of the class.

Doug's version of the course allowed him to negotiate an acceptable identity in the face of seemingly contradictory evidence. By creating an understanding of Robert's course that allowed a reasonable person to "opt out," Doug made his failing grades *not* mean that he was a poor student or that he did not belong in college. Instead, his understanding cast Robert and himself in a separate but equal relationship—they understood each other, respected each other, but chose to disagree about the importance of being a writer. Such a stance meant, of course, that Doug did belong in college, could think as well as Robert could, and just needed a different course to fulfill his writing requirement. It was a way of understanding his experience that protected his identity as someone who belongs in college.

Susan

Unlike Doug, Susan had high expectations for the course and found herself frustrated by her experience. In her initial self-evaluation, Susan explained that she intended to get a Ph.D. in child psychology and that her goal for her first year was to make the dean's list. She went on to describe her typical writing experience:

> When I am writing I like to get all the main ideas out and use my creativity. This results in somewhat of a mess because my mechanics and punctuation are awful. I have always done well in english because of my style and imagination but when it came down to the mechanics I have always needed a great deal of help . . . It is frustrating for me to get back a paper that says "excellent work." Susan [sic] but then read further and see in red ink, need's [sic] work on punctuation and format. It doesn't come easy for me. But I am more determined then [sic] ever to succeed. (Unedited student text)

Susan entered the course, by her own admission, with high motivation to succeed in college and more mechanical difficulty than the average Minnesota first year student. By the time she left the course, she had become successful in writing papers for Robert but had also become dissatisfied with the whole experience, being relatively sure that Robert was idiosyncratic and that she was not learning anything useful.

In light of Susan's experience, her response was not extreme. Of the four students in her small group, Susan was the only one to be sent to the Writing Lab for extra help with her mechanics. Her experience with her tutor in the Writing Lab highlighted in her mind the unusual nature of Robert's course. During her third meeting with her tutor, she found out that the tutor did not understand Robert's assignment either, since he had never heard of issue trees and collages as exploration devices. Susan arranged a meeting with both Robert and the tutor in which they agreed that Robert himself would tutor her, since the tutor had not worked with these tools before. As Susan described it, from that point on she got high marks on her papers, "but then *he* wrote my papers."

In the taped interview with her group, she described her strategy as "giving the teacher what he wants" for the purpose of a good grade, but explained that she would abandon this style of writing as soon as the course was over:

> He tells me how to do them, I do them exactly the way he wants them. I'm getting good grades, but that isn't the way I'd write my papers, so I—

I'm afraid that I don't know what's going to happen when I get *out* of the
class, 'cause I won't keep writing my papers the way *he* wants them—
(Excerpt from small group interview, appendix 1)

Although Susan worried about whether Robert's expectations would
transfer to other college classes ("I don't know what's going to happen"), she had pretty well decided that Robert was an anomaly and
did not need to be taken seriously. As she described it, "only *he*
knows what he wants" (appendix 1): "Well he-he knows exactly what
he wants to see, and if he doesn't see it, he's like a little *kid* and
you're the one that suffers."

Susan produced a judgment of the course that protected her
sense of self as motivated student in the face of negative response.
Where Doug could separate himself entirely from the class because
he didn't want to succeed at what was offered, Susan was deeply
challenged because she wanted very much to succeed as a writer
and college student. Her response to the class defended this sense
of self—she decided that Robert was not typical of college people
and that her experience here did not count. He was odd, so her lack
of success didn't reflect on her ability—it reflected on him.

For Susan, Robert's focus on audience was misguided, since in
her experience audience was obvious—the audience is the teacher:
"I think *audience* is going to be *obvious*, I mean if you're writing a,
um, the only person that has to read it really is your pro*fess*or, I
mean that—it's *obvious* that you're writing it to him" (appendix 1).
The audience is the direct evaluator, the teacher who gives the
grade. For Susan, the course made this point very clear. She had
never had a teacher like Robert before, and his differences from
other teachers highlighted for her that different teachers have different expectations, and the only standard is the need to give teachers
what they want. Susan spent a great deal of time during the taped
interview, for example, complaining about how different this course
was from those her peers had and about how different those courses
were from one another. For her, this confirmed her belief that "the
audience is the teacher."

Even so, Susan's firm belief that the only one she had to please
was Robert, and her firm sense that Robert was significantly different from other teachers, did not get in the way of her scholastic success. She was able to bend her writing to Robert's requirements and

ended up with a "B" in the course, a mark of relative success. Although she never internalized the concept of audience as Robert thought he was teaching it, she was able to figure out what he wanted in her papers and notebook, and deliver it. She was frustrated throughout the course because she felt he was hiding his specific requirements from the class (she was convinced he had specific requirements for form, content, etc.), but she nevertheless was able to produce successful work in Robert's eyes.

Her overall response to the course, then, was to interpret the concept of audience as the individual evaluating one's writing (in this case, Robert), and to classify Robert's evaluations as odd, atypical, and useless for her future life as a college student. She didn't buy, in other words, Robert's relationship to students as a fellow writer or his relationship to them as diagnostician. Like any teacher, he was just an authority who demanded students perform tasks and then evaluated tasks according to some criteria he had. As a teacher, he was lousy because he did not make his criteria clear. For Susan, this was the reality of her experience; the rest was gravy.

Like Doug's response, Susan's response to the course negotiated a stance toward the class that supported her sense of self. Like Doug, she also chose to distance herself from many of the relationships Robert developed in the class, and, like Doug, she took this stance in order to preserve a positive sense of self in the face of negative feedback. Unlike Doug, however, she could not see Robert as an authority about writing—for her to maintain her sense of self as a successful writer, as a student who was going to be a successful academic, Robert had to be seen as merely an arbitrary authority, as an aberration from other college people, as an example of a poor teacher. Her learning, thus, was completely colored by her need to protect her conception of herself—she left rejecting the course entirely, both teacher and ideas, because this stance toward the course allowed her to maintain her conceptions of self in the face of negative feedback.

George

The story of George's progress through the course is the story of a sea-change. At first, George was extremely frustrated, but by the end of the quarter he had become the foremost defender of Robert's ideas. He was able, we think, to join together his writing practice with the concept of audience Robert taught, and, consequently, found a strong sense of identity as "good student and writer."

For the first four weeks, George was the most vocal and seemingly most frustrated member of the class. He repeatedly grilled Robert for more explicit instructions during class, after class, and during office hours. He got lower marks than he wanted on his papers and consistently asked for clarification of "What You Want." Then, suddenly, in the middle of the fifth week, George changed. He started getting good grades (at one point, Robert told him he had written "the best paper in the class"), began to help explain assignments to other students, and began to act relatively happy in class. When the observer asked his group to give their responses to the class, he was the first to volunteer, and it was exactly on this change that he focused:

> I like it. *Now.* But it was really confusing at first, it was really confusing at first, I didn't like it at all. Then, once I—once I saw what he was trying to do and stuff, makes sense. Makes more sense than other teachers who they just concentrate on spelling and stuff like that. He concentrates on what's in your writing not on spelling and stuff like that—audience and stuff like—'Cause you can use that when you get out of, when you get out of that class, you have to write to a certain audience and stuff, you know how to write to an audience. (Excerpt from small group interview, appendix 1)

For George, the change in his response to the class was in part due to an entirely new conceptualization of the course. He began, it seems, understanding the course very much like Susan had, as a response to a single teacher with specific requirements. What changed, we think, is that midway through the course George understood the concept of audience as Robert was trying to explain it and suddenly saw the course as one example of how readership influences writing. He could then accept a relationship to Robert as fellow writer because he now understood how to do the tasks before him. He could also accept a relationship to Robert as diagnostician because he felt he had advanced in his thinking about writing.

For George, the idea of audience as a tool for writing seemed an incredible insight, and he repeatedly tried to defend his positive experience with the course on the basis of his understanding of audience. In fact, in one place during the discussion, he used this idea to counter an argument from Kris and Susan that Robert's requirements were anomalous:

> *Kris:* Other teachers aren't going to want what Robert wants, so we should—
> *George: Well that's the whole thing!* You, that's kind of what's good about this class, you, he's *different*, so you got to figure out what he wants, so other teachers—
> *Kris:* I know, but—
> *George:* You'll be able to figure out what *they* want.
> (Excerpt from small group interview, appendix 1)

For George, the experience in this course taught him something generalizable, something he would be able to use in other courses and other writing situations —and this something is "audience." Throughout the interview, he kept coming back to this point, defending the course, claiming he was making progress, extolling the virtues of audience, until Susan at one point exclaimed "You said that already ten times!" We sensed that George felt he had worked hard for his insight and found it tremendously useful, and that he was frustrated with the way Susan and Kris were responding to the course. His repeated defenses of his experience seemed an attempt to prove that his understanding of audience was insightful, that he was developing, and that Robert was not "just weird," as Susan was arguing. In the most remarkable incident on tape, close to the end of the interview, George suddenly turned to the interviewer and asked:

> *George:* Is [Robert] working for his doctorate?
> *Interviewer:* Yup. He's in the midst of writing his dissertation.
> *George:* So he's just about a professor, huh?
> *Susan:* God help us all.
> *George:* [to Susan and Kris] *See!*
> *Kris:* Hanhh! [gasp].
> (Excerpt from small group interview, appendix 1)

George seemed to be seeking some kind of outside verification of his experience here, outside support for his sense that this was a good class. In the series of questions and comments that followed, George pushed for more and more information about Robert and used the information he got to support his opinions with a quiet but forceful "See" directed toward his skeptic peers. It had become very important to George to prove that Robert knew what he was talking about because he wanted to hold on to his sense of his own development in the class:

Interviewer: "See!" What do you mean, "See!"?

George: He probably knows how—he probably knows how to write more than you do.

Doug: Yeah, of *course* he does—

Susan: Yeah, but he knows how to write the way he wants to write, but the way he was taught to write—

George: [to interviewer] What do *you* think of him as a writer?

Susan: I was not taught to write that way.

Kris: He—he's teaching us—

Interviewer: What do I think of him as a writer?

George: Yeah.

Interviewer: Well, I—

Susan: [chuckles]

Interviewer: I've read some of his finished work, and I think that it's extremely lucid, very insightful, um, he's a very—

George: Hunh!

Interviewer: able writer, *I* think. Uh, for audiences like me.

(3 second pause)

George: For audiences like the other *college* people?

(2 second pause)

Interviewer: Yeah. I mean I, I would be, I would be an academic audience, and the writing that I've seen of his for that audience. I've seen, for example I'm in a conference group with Robert, um, that we discuss people's dissertation chapters and so forth, so I've seen a number of the chapters from Robert's dissertation.

George: What is a dissertation, a *book?*

Interviewer: [coughs] Basically.

George: On how to *write*, or what?

Interviewer: Uh, Ph.D. dissertations are concentrated in depth studies, uh, in specific areas of interest. It's a way to demonstrate academically that you have control of a subject in depth, and Robert's is on, uh, composition *theory*, theories of how people, uh, produce written discourse. (2 second pause)

George: Is he using the ideas in his dissertation on us?

Interviewer: Uhh, I think that, that, *I* see, from what I've read of his stuff, *yes*—

George: [to women] See.

(Excerpt from small group interview, appendix 1)

Throughout this passage, George pushes the interviewer for information that will prove Robert knows what he is talking about. He pushes to find out (1) that Robert is an able writer; (2) that college people like Robert's writing; (3) that Robert is writing a "book" on writing; and (4) that the ideas in this "book" are being taught in Robert's classroom. This chain of information is all aimed at establishing that Robert knows what he is doing, so that George's sense of the class and his experience can be confirmed. George, in other words, went to great lengths to prove to himself and his classmates that his sense of himself as a learner and writer was valid. He needed to defend his position as one who understood Robert's ideas and improved his writing abilities as a consequence. In short, for George to maintain a sense of himself as someone who learned in this classroom, he needed to establish Robert as a real authority on writing (teacher as diagnostician) because then his own success in the classroom established him as someone who "developed more than others."

Like the other students, then, George's stance toward the course—and towards other students—was motivated by a need to support his sense of himself (in this case, as a good student who is developing). His reactions and questions serve to position himself in relation to Robert, the observer, his peers, and college people in ways that increase his sense of self-importance. Although the negotiations he used to achieve this end are radically different from Susan's or Doug's, he too experienced the course in ways that allowed him to work out an acceptable, positive sense of self in this environment.

Kris

Kris's experience in the course is most typical of the class as a whole. Her reaction was decidedly ambivalent—she saw the point to much of what happened but felt completely frustrated much of the time. Hence her belief that she was learning something, but that something was wrong:

> *Kris:* I'm not saying that what he's teaching is bad. At all, I mean I—
> *George:* Just the way he's doing it?
> *Kris:* Yeah.
> (Excerpt from small group interview, appendix 1)

In her initial self-evaluation, Kris described herself as someone who loved to write, whose father was an author, and who had done well in Advanced Placement English her senior year of high school. For these reasons, she was sure composition was going to be her easiest class. As the course progressed, however, Kris found herself more and more frustrated because she could not seem to get the grades she wanted, and she felt more and more that she could not get those grades because she was unable to get inside Robert's head to see what he wanted. This made her response to the course completely ambivalent. Like George, she liked many of the ideas in the course; like Susan, she thought Robert was idiosyncratic and dictatorial:

> I don't like—I mean I like—the, like George said, the things that he did were great, working with audience and stuff like that, and, you know, *not* just working with spelling, but I don't like the way he grades at all— because I think that if you don't do exactly what he had in mind, that, he'll give you a bad grade.
> (Excerpt from small group interview, appendix 1)

As the course progressed, Kris's frustration over not getting high grades made it harder for her to like the course and easier for her to reject it as odd. During the group interview, Kris consequently seemed like a tennis ball, bouncing between George and Susan, agreeing with one, then agreeing with the other, not seeming to notice her self-contradiction. Like George, she wanted to claim she had learned something and was a better writer; like Susan, she wanted to claim she was a good student in the face of negative feedback from Robert. Hence the contradiction. She wanted both implied identities, the identity of successful learner and the identity of good student, and her experience in Robert's course put these self-conceptions into conflict. Consider the contradiction involved in the following two excerpts:

> *George:* I mean, you know how to evaluate the audience, you know how to write for them, you know what they want—
> *Kris:* In your way of—I think that's important.
> *George:* You know, how to find out what they want and stuff like that. I *never* did *that* before.
> (2 second pause)
> *Kris:* Well, 'cause my dad—I know that's true because my dad's, my dad's um, he writes a, he's an editor of a newspaper and he writes an article for the weekend. He, you know, he just—*he has to be* aware of who he's writing to, and, I mean it's *true*. He's *not* just writing to a teacher, he's writing to, you know, whoever's going to read the paper.
> (Excerpt from small group interview, appendix 1)

> *Susan:* Then how are you, you know, how are you going to know if we been doing it right, because he's so—
> *Kris:* I know, but, you know, other classes maybe you only have to write one paper, so you're just going to have to *do* it however, you know, and *Robert* is just trying to teach us to write, you know, *his* way, but maybe other teachers aren't going to like that so you should just—he should *help* you figure out what *you* want to write—
> (Excerpt from small group interview, appendix 1)

In the first excerpt, Kris agrees with George that audience is a true and useful concept; in the second, she agrees with Susan that Robert is teaching *his* way to write, and it probably isn't anybody else's way to write. Kris sits on the fence, sure only that she's frustrated, with a whirl of audience- and identity-related items swirling around in her head: evaluate the audience, find a readership, please the teacher, what does he want, why did I get "C," who is my audience and what will Robert think of this, does his opinion even count, why is he so weird, I know I'm a good writer why doesn't he see it? To claim that Kris understood what Robert was trying to teach, or to claim that she did not, would be to miss half her experience, for in her experience she both found some importance in the concept of audience and felt unable to figure out Robert as an audience for her compositions—she experienced, we could claim, the full confusion that results from the coming together of the teacher-student relationships in Robert's classroom. The result may be learning, since George, Doug, and Kris all claimed they learned, but the result is certainly frustration and tension, which each student exhibited in a different way.

The way each student came to understand the course's tensions, thus, produced a different view of the value of the course and their own identities in relation to it. Some students, like Doug, separated themselves completely from the course, refusing to let what happened there implicate them at all. Others, like George and Susan, took a strong stance toward the course, thereby defending their own sense of themselves as students, writers, and learners. Still others, like Kris, found themselves taking several stances toward the course, being finally unsure whether their experience in it was valid and whether they were better writers or poorer students as a consequence. The identities of all of these students were changed or threatened in some way by their experience, and the stance they took regarding the course significantly reflected the sense of self they wanted to preserve.

3

Conclusions and Implications

IN THE LAST CHAPTER, WE PRESENTED A DETAILED DESCRIPTION of one first year writing class. We described the teacher's ideas, the ongoing activities, and the reactions of several students to this class. In this chapter, we will reflect on what this description suggests for research and teaching in composition, focusing especially on the general problem of learning to write for an audience.

This study began with a pedagogical question: what happens when we teach "writing to an audience" in an instructional setting where teachers, and not the addressed audience, assign the grades? From our investigation of this class, we believe we have found a partial answer to that question: what happens is that students and teacher will negotiate understandings of their classroom experience that support their senses of self, and these negotiations will influence their responses to the idea of audience. These negotiations involve issues of group membership. Classroom participants negotiate a sense of self largely by positioning themselves in relation to important social groups in the classroom and the surrounding institution.

George, Susan, Doug, and Kris all showed this process of negotiation. During the course of the quarter, George came to see "writing to an audience" as something successful college writers do. Since he wanted to be included in this group, he applauded his experience in this course. Doug also found Robert's way of writing clearly appropriate for those who want to be writers—but since he did not want to be a writer, the course really didn't mean anything to him. Susan, in contrast to George and Doug, came to perceive "writing to an audience" as merely one of Robert's weird demands. Since she perceived Robert as unrepresentative of the group of college people she wanted to join, she rejected this demand. Finally, Kris found herself frustrated and unsure of her experience. Like George and Doug, she saw "writing to an audience" as something good writers do; like George, she wanted to belong to that group. But she, like Susan, also felt that Robert's demands were potentially unrepresentative of other college teachers and that his ideas might not help her become successful in college. In all these cases, student understanding of class concepts was influenced by the way they positioned themselves in relation to the social groups they saw operating in and around the classroom.

In short, we found that students dealt with the conflicts in this particular writing class by working to negotiate an acceptable sense of the sort of people they were and the sort of groups they belonged to. This negotiation, instead of any explicit concern with learning audience awareness, was what motivated their classroom behavior. In fact, each student developed an understanding of class activities and concepts largely through these negotiations, and the students' negotiations influenced their understanding of the class.

What we found in this class may be generally true of most educational interactions. A large motivator of student behavior is the potential for individual membership in (and alignment toward) important social groups. How classroom behaviors help individuals "fit in" to desired groups is what often seems most important to participants. Hence, how individuals act in class is greatly motivated by their sense of the group memberships available in each classroom. Students are not merely in class to learn material; more importantly, they are in class to become members of groups they value and to learn how to act so that these groups recognize them as one of their own.

This motivation may have been easier to see in this class than many others because we expected to see conflicts between the teacher's demands and the demands of students' own audiences (and thus were prepared to look for group membership conflicts). But the kinds of interactions we found should occur in any classroom. The crucial problems of membership and alignment always exist, although, no doubt, in different ways in different classrooms.

In this chapter, we will consequently step back from the minute particulars of the course we studied to suggest general implications of this way of looking at writing and learning. Such theorizing, of course, involves speculating in advance of our data, but we believe such theory is relevant to many issues writing teachers and researchers discuss.

In particular, we will (1) address the learning of audience awareness from the perspective this study allows; (2) suggest some general dynamics of learning and negotiation that researchers should investigate; (3) speculate on ways teachers could use a knowledge of these dynamics to improve the teaching of writing. In all of these cases, we will draw on data from our study, but our goal will be to develop theory rather than to account for every particular.

Audience, Student Behavior, and Negotiation

Participant-observation studies have a way of making researchers reconsider what they take for granted. As we suggested in the first chapter, one of the virtues of borrowing ethnographic research methods is that they allow researchers to compare cultural experiences. Researchers can stand on the boundary between the "home" and the "studied" communities and use this boundary position to develop insights important to both. In relation to the idea of teaching audience awareness, our study has forced us into such a position.

We began our study with a very "teacherly" question: how can we teach audience in the institutional setting of college classrooms? In asking this question, we assumed all sorts of things that our community, the community of writing teachers, takes for granted. Among these assumptions were that students are in class primarily to learn, that the content teachers teach and test is what guides learning, and that the accumulation of knowledge and skills is what classroom interaction is mainly about. As teachers, we use these assumptions every time we plan a course or develop curricular goals. In our community, such ideas influence what we think of as the basic purpose for our courses.

Our study allowed us to see one writing classroom from the perspective of another community, the loose community of first year students. Even though we teachers share with first year students many cultural values, ideas, and behaviors, our experience of classrooms is remarkably different. For the students we studied, the idea of learning audience awareness was not the primary goal of their classroom behavior. Nor, in fact, was their primary goal the more general improvement of writing knowledge and skills. In the experience of the students we studied, each of these goals was secondary to other, more important goals.

Foremost for these students were issues of whether or not they belonged in college and, if they did, where and how they belonged there. At issue was their individual membership in the social groups college represents—groups of educated professionals; groups of white-collar as opposed to blue-collar workers; groups of self-sufficient adults as opposed to dependents and children. What was at stake for these students was *not* how much knowledge and skills about writing they added to their repertoires. Instead, they were most concerned with what their behavior in this class meant about their membership in these important groups. Gaining greater control over audience or writing was important only as *part* of the more general goal of positioning themselves in relation to these groups.

In short, our initial question appeared later, in many ways, to be the wrong question to ask. The question should have been "what sort of person will learning the concept of audience help students become?" or "what sort of groups will the behaviors in our class help students enter?" Before the study started, we had expected to focus on the development of students' writing knowledge and processes as they passed through this course. We found instead a more crucial focus on students' self-understanding and sense of membership in the groups college represents. Each student's senses of self and group membership guided that student's actions in (and interpretations of) the class. The knowledge and processes they developed in writing only became relevant as they connected to these senses.

The students we described in chapter 2 exemplify the way group membership guided the understanding and use of audience awareness. George came to understand audience awareness as something college people use in writing because this understanding enabled him to assert his membership in a perceived group of advanced college writers. Doug chose to get a "D" (and take the class again with another teacher) because he saw a difference between writers and college people, and he wanted a course that would help him become a member of the latter group without his having to join the former. For him, audience awareness (and the other writing techniques

Robert presented) were important to writers, but were not neces-
sary for the particular groups of college people he wanted to join.
Susan saw audience awareness as the arbitrary desire of a single, unrepresentative teacher, because this understanding allowed her to
assert her membership in the college mainstream even though she
didn't get along with her writing teacher. For each of these students,
what motivated their understanding of the course was what they felt
this classroom experience showed about their membership in the
groups they desired to enter.

In other words, although the concept of audience is tremendously
important for composition theorists and teachers, in the experience
of student writers, understanding the concept is not an end in itself.
In fact, it may be that for students, no knowledge, concept, or skill
is an end in itself, no matter what our behavioral objectives might
be or what cultural literacy we intend to develop.

What is more important is how students use classroom interaction
to negotiate their growing sense of self as members in the social
groups they want to enter. What our study suggests, in other words,
is that in studying writers' composing processes and rhetorical knowledge, composition researchers have been looking at only a part of the
actual dynamics of learning to write. This study suggests that we step
back and place student writers' processes and knowledge in a larger
context: the development and negotiation of individual identities in
a complex social environment. The behaviors of writing (and learning to write) are part of the behavior that goes into this larger negotiation, and only when we understand that negotiation can we really
understand the writing behaviors we have been uncovering for the
last twenty years.

Learning and Identity Negotiation: Directions for Research

Our study provides a window into some of the dynamics of writing
classrooms. Overall, it suggests that a crucial factor in classroom
interaction is the identity negotiations of participants. By negotiating the distances between implied identities in the classroom and
participants' own senses of membership in certain social groups, students (and teacher) position their classroom experience in relation
to their felt identities, their senses of the sort of people they are.

In the class we studied, such negotiations strongly influenced students' understanding of course concepts and activities. The quality and kind of each student's identity negotiations determined that student's understanding of the course. A great part of classroom behavior—including the behaviors we like to think of as learning—was influenced by such negotiations.

For researchers in composition, this potential connection between students' identity negotiations and their learning is important. Composition researchers have developed many descriptions of *how* writers write, of the differences between experienced writers' behavior and students' behavior, and of the growth of students' writing in many contexts. What the connection between identity negotiation and learning allows, however, is a partial explanation of *why* students behave the way they do in writing classrooms. The idea of identity negotiation suggests ways of explaining why some students learn writing faster than others, why some students resist writing, and why others succeed at some writing tasks and fail at others. Identity negotiation allows us to get at the motivation behind writing behavior in classrooms; it thus extends our knowledge of the complexities of writing and learning.

Our study primarily showed that identity negotiation influences how students understand their classroom experience. The ways students positioned themselves relative to college people, Robert, and the other students influenced the ways they understood the course. George, for example, liked what he had learned in the course because he perceived both himself and Robert as belonging to a group of successful college writers. Susan, on the other hand, felt she had learned nothing because she perceived Robert as outside the group of college people she was trying to enter and found his agenda arbitrary and idiosyncratic. Obviously, these students' understanding of their learning was influenced by their identity negotiations within Robert's class.

Although our study did establish a connection between student learning and identity negotiation, it did not establish exactly what kind of connection exists. Future research in writing classrooms could help to illuminate this connection. Given the preliminary and speculative nature of our study, many important questions remain unanswered. We will address two sets of these questions here, focusing on what needs to be known about learning and identity negotiation in particular.

Learning

It is not clear from our study exactly what is involved in student learning. This term may cover many different activities and hence needs to be examined more carefully.

Consider, for example, the great difference between George's and Susan's activities in class. George left feeling he had learned a great deal; Susan left feeling she had learned nothing. As we have shown, these responses connect rather directly with very different patterns of identity negotiation within the classroom.

Yet, at the same time, there was not a tremendous difference between the grades these students received or the work they were doing. George received an "A" in the course; Susan received a "B." Both wrote papers by the end of the semester that satisfied Robert's demands. Their learning, as measured by the criteria of grades and work performed, did not differ as greatly as their own accounts of their learning did.

What exactly, then, is meant by "learning"? Does "learning" mean performance as measured by grades or work? Does it mean the students' own sense of the usefulness of what they experience in class? Or does it mean something else entirely?

Most often, when researchers speak of learning they mean some kind of *change* in skills, concepts, knowledge, or attitudes—and often these changes are not held to be found in any simple way in what people say or don't say about them. Our study did not collect data to show if students' skills, concepts, etc., actually did change during the quarter; instead, we collected a number of students' reactions to their first year college writing course. Our study, thus, collected data about the *experience* of students rather than about any direct changes in skills or concepts. As researchers, we need to think carefully about the ways student experience really connects with student learning, especially when identity negotiations of the sort we found are also going on.

It may be that learning involves two radically different sets of changes in a person. On the one hand, learning may involve changes in skills, concepts, and knowledge, as is often assumed. Such learning might be thought of as simple addition of material or processes to a person's "mental memory banks"—as a consequence of learning, a person has more "stuff" in her repertoire. But, on the other hand, perhaps the students' descriptions of their learning points to something different. Learning may also involve connecting a new skill or concept to one's sense of social behavior. When a new skill or concept is perceived as enabling a person to behave in ways that bring social approval from key social groups, that skill or concept is understood as learning; when a skill is not believed to enable such behavior, it is understood as a waste of time. When we think of learning to write we tend to mean both kinds of changes. We mean both the accumulation of new skills and concepts and the recognition that these new skills enable the acquisition of desired social approval.

It is the second aspect of learning that our study began to address. Basically, students' identity negotiations influenced their understanding of how this class's concepts and skills might lead to desired social approval. Through the ways they positioned themselves toward the class and other groups of college people, students developed an understanding of the usefulness of the course material. We do not know from the collected data if students really added new skills or concepts to their mental memory banks as a consequence of taking the course. What we do know is how students understood the course material and its usefulness for their college lives.

The students' understanding of their course experience, however, seemed to them much more important than any simple addition of new knowledge. This aspect of their learning is what would prompt them to welcome or fear more writing classes or to want to try techniques from this class in other classes. This is what led Doug to take the course over and George to argue that this course was better than other writing courses he had had. It was the students' understanding of the implications of course materials for their future social lives that determined what they felt they learned from the course. And their understandings of the course came, as we have shown, from identity negotiations.

All of this suggests that in investigating learning composition researchers need to focus more attention on students' identity negotiations, on the ways students come to understand the social significance of their classroom behaviors for their social selves. The kinds of learning we are most interested in when we investigate learning to write may well be the kinds that are wrapped up with identity negotiations.

In calling for research on learning through identity negotiations, we are leaving open and problematic the relationship between learning in the sense of addition of new skills or knowledge and learning in the sense of self-perceived improvement or enablement. This relationship is also in need of study, largely because it questions our accepted notions of intellectual development in learning.

In recent years, a dominant and fashionable way of accounting for changes in students' knowledge and skills (learning in sense 1 above) has been to posit different stages of intellectual development. Drawing on the work of Piaget (1950) and Perry (1970), researchers have argued that young writers need to develop through several stages of radically different intellectual functioning before they can write effectively. According to this argument, beginning writers tend to think egocentrically, concretely, and dualistically—they are bound by a too rigid focus on their own experience and are unable to separate an object of thought from that experience in order to investigate it from a number of different perspectives. In the course of their college years, students are believed to develop from a stage of egocentrism or dualism to a more advanced stage of decentralized, formal operational, relativistic thought. This "higher" stage of intellectual functioning supposedly allows the student to take herself out of the blinders imposed by her own experience and to manipulate thoughts and ideas easily from many perspectives. Several composition researchers have argued that the crucial skills of task definition and audience analysis in writing require such a shift in intellectual stages of development and that students' stages of development are thus a useful predictor of their success on writing tasks (see Lunsford 1979; Bizzell 1984; Bereiter 1980).

This way of accounting for "writing development" seems straightforward and clear as long as researchers are only focusing on learning in sense 1 above: as an addition of new knowledge, skills, or processes to exisiting repertoires. It seems less straightforward, however, when learning in sense 2 is added to the picture. The notion of learning as a self-perceived improvement or enablement would ask us to investigate how any given change in skills/knowledge/processes allows students to improve their interactions in their social environment. It might suggest, in contrast to the hypothesis that "my students can't do my assignments because they're at a lower stage of intellectual development," that student resistance to assigned work occurs because students cannot perceive any direct improvement for themselves from doing that work. Perhaps students resist assignments that are supposedly too difficult because it is not clear to them how those assignments will enable them to achieve greater social approval outside the classroom. Perhaps what we perceive as evidence of stages of development when we look only at learning as a change in skills/knowledge might appear to be evidence of a clash of social expectations if we looked at learning as a felt sense of enablement.

At this point, the question remains open. We recognize that "developmental stages" and "conflict and negotiation" are competing hypotheses for explaining student behavior, and we do not think that our study really allows any final rejection of one hypothesis in favor of the other. We do think, however, that our study may problematize the developmental stage hypothesis. Our students did not seem to focus on dualistic/relativistic problems or concrete/formal operational problems in their accounts of the course, but rather on the presumed usefulness of their experience for their social lives. Identity negotiations amidst classroom conflicts thus seem more descriptive of what we found—but then, we were looking for such negotiations. Further research—with students of different ages, in different contexts, with different "measured" developmental stages—might make the relative explanatory adequacy of the two hypotheses clear. We expect such research would find that identity negotiations in classroom settings largely guide or motivate what we have understood as developmental stages, but at present this expectation is just our opinion and needs further investigation.

Identity Negotiations

This suggestion brings up another set of questions. What exactly are the identity negotiations that lead to students' understanding of their classroom experience? Our study shows that students generally negotiate understandings of their classroom experience that support their senses of self, but it does not address in any significant way the range of possible negotiations, the methods by which they work, or the reasons they work some ways and not others. Further research is needed here as well; in fact, given the preliminary and hypothesis-generating nature of our study, we can only claim to have identified these negotiations as something researchers should study.

The general idea of identity negotiations seems to account for much of the behavior in the classroom we studied. But we expect this general idea will take many forms. There may be many kinds of identity negotiation, each following its own patterns and arising in different contexts. As researchers of writing and education, we need to work to understand the dynamics of identity negotiation more thoroughly.

For example, students in Robert's class exhibited at least two very different kinds of identity negotiation. One set of students negotiated their relationship to class in a way that effectively maintained their previous feelings about themselves. Another set of students appeared to change some of their feelings about themselves through their negotiations. This suggests that there may be a difference between "maintenance" identity negotiations and "alteration" or "formation" identity negotiations. If differences like these exist, there are probably others that our study did not uncover.

The difference between negotiations aimed at identity maintenance and negotiations aimed at identity alteration appears most clearly in the reactions of Doug and Susan on the one hand and George on the other. Doug and Susan both negotiated a way of understanding their classroom experience that resisted or precluded any change in their future behavior. George, in contrast, claimed to change his understanding of successful writers as a consequence of the course and claimed to change his own behavior accordingly.

Doug is perhaps the clearest case of identity maintenance negotiations. Doug built a distinction between writers and other college students in order to believe that he could be a successful college student without having to try any of the techniques his writing teacher suggested. He entered the course asserting that he did not want to be a writer, and, even though he claimed to understand the importance of his teacher's ideas for writers, he negotiated an understanding of the class that maintained both his dislike for writing and his sense of himself as a successful college student. Doug's negotiations in the course, thus, seemed largely aimed at working out a way to maintain the feelings he already held about himself as a student and a writer in a context where other implications about his identity were present.

Susan, similarly, negotiated a position toward the course that largely preserved her original sense of self. She entered the course highly committed to being a successful college student and academic. Her negotiations during class served to preserve this sense of self in the face of negative feedback from her teacher. By coming to see Robert as unrepresentative of mainstream college teachers, she could understand her classroom experience as only an example of the arbitrariness of teachers. Her disagreement with Robert's ideas, therefore, did not mean she was unsuccessful. Her understanding of the class experience, thus, primarily served to maintain her sense of self in the face of potentially contradictory feedback.

In both of these cases, the students worked to mitigate a perceived dissonance between their felt identity and the implied identities of the classroom. Both students felt they were the sort of people who belong in college but found (in different ways) that their classroom experience implied otherwise. Thus, in order to maintain their felt identity as college people they negotiated ways of understanding the implications of the writing class that mitigated the dissonance. Doug's distinction between writers and college people and Susan's understanding of Robert as unrepresentative of most college professors served to bring implied identity in line with felt identity, to negotiate the potential dissonance between the two.

In contrast to Doug and Susan, George's pattern of negotiations during the class was very different. Rather than negotiate a way of remaining the same, George explicitly claimed that he had learned something and that he was better off as a consequence of Robert's course. In describing his experience, George focused on a change in his perception. At first, he was frustrated and unsure; then, halfway through the course, he understood Robert, and suddenly realized that Robert's ideas would help him become a more successful writer. By the end of the course, George was vigorously defending his class experience as better than his other writing courses. He felt, as a consequence of this course, that he "understood audience" and could now write successfully for any audience he might face.

During the course, in short, George seemed to change his notion of what a successful writer does. He apparently decided that his earlier understanding of successful writers was faulty and that the way of understanding presented in this course was better. It seems that George restructured part of his felt identity to include elements of the implied identities operating in his classroom. He entered the course feeling he was a potentially successful college student and left still feeling he was successful, but now describing what makes a successful college writer using vocabulary introduced by the course. The implied identity of a successful writer as someone who understands audience had somehow become a part of George's felt identity of successful college student. Because he had succeeded at what the class implied, he felt he was that much more the sort of person he wanted to be.

Where Doug and Susan negotiated a way of eliminating the dissonance between their felt and their implied identities, George negotiated a way of making his implied identity part of his felt identity. These are very different patterns of negotiation, with very different results. In the first case, the negotiations served to enable the students to resist feeling they learned anything from the course; in the second case, the negotiations served to connect course material to the student's self-understanding. The way these students will behave in the future would seem to be very much connected to these patterns of negotiation.

The patterns of negotiation these students exhibit are, of course, only two possible patterns. There are potentially a number of other such patterns, many of which may influence student learning as significantly as these patterns do. As composition theorists and researchers, we need to understand the possible scope and purpose of such negotiations in a wide range of educational settings. In the class we studied, the patterns of identity negotiations greatly influenced how students understood and used the course material and seemingly influenced what they learned as well. We expect that such identity negotiations influence student understanding and learning in classes generally. But, from this one study, there is no reason to expect that all classes will involve the same kinds of negotiations, or that negotiations will serve the same purposes in all contexts.

The negotiations in the class we studied emerged from complex teacher-student relationships and the frustration and confusion these relationships engendered. Other classes will have other conflicts that are more dominant and in which the teacher-student relationships play a lesser part. We can imagine classes where factions between student groups cause more stress, or where outside institutional expectations (like upcoming placement or exit exams) hang over the whole class. In such classes, we would expect radically different kinds of negotiation, leading potentially to radically different senses of learning. As a profession, teachers need to understand the dynamics of classroom negotiation much more thoroughly, for such understanding will help us account for the motivation of student behavior and student learning. Our study identifies such negotiations as something that needs to be investigated; it is only the first of a number of studies we need to conduct to understand the phenomena thoroughly.

Implied Identities and Classroom Communities: Implications for Teaching

We see two major implications for teaching from our study. The first involves the recognition that forms of identity negotiation are always a part of classroom interaction. The second involves some speculation about how the concept of audience might be more successfully presented in writing classes.

First, teachers generally need to recognize that teaching is probably always involved in the kinds of wider classroom dynamics our class exhibited. Teaching, we expect, always creates implied identities for students and teachers, and often creates the kinds of multiple and conflicting relationships this class produced. We would especially expect such conflicts to occur in experimental classes where teachers are trying new strategies or trying to bring new ideas and theories into classroom practice. Such a situation creates the possibility for mixed and conflicting teacher-student relationships, since experimental teaching often involves an attempt to work out and create new roles, new implied identities, for teacher and students. The kinds of conflicting relationships created in the class we studied, thus, may be just "part of the territory" of exploring new teaching techniques. This in itself is useful knowledge for teachers.

But another aspect of this point is also useful. Much of the success or failure of any teaching practice depends on the ways that practice creates implied identities and the ways that practice handles potential conflicts that may arise over identity implications. Each method of teaching carries implied identities with it, and teachers would do well to think about what their own methods imply. The central question in evaluating the effectiveness of teaching, in fact, may well not be "what content and skills am I teaching?" as much as "what range of implied identities is my teaching practice providing?" Thinking in terms of students' identity negotiations may be a more effective way of thinking about teaching.

Our second implication involves the teaching of audience itself. Obviously, as our study shows, the very idea of teaching "writing to an audience" in a classroom setting is fraught with difficulty. We do not see how any such teaching can help but present students with conflicting demands. One useful implication of our study, then, is simply this: teaching "writing to an audience" always presents real conflicts to students in writing classrooms. We need to be aware of this in order to deal with these conflicts effectively.

But the fact that these conflicts exist does not mean they need to become as big a problem for students as they did for the students in our study. Here we can only speculate again, but it would seem that one could overcome many of these problems by introducing audience only after a strong "sense of community" had developed in the classroom. If the problem in Robert's class was that students were never sure how to define themselves in relation to the teacher and the college community, then creating a strong sense of membership in the classroom, a strong sense of supportive implied identities, might help. If students felt secure in their classroom positions before being asked to confront the conflicts inherent in "writing to an audience," then they might not find themselves as frustrated and worried as Robert's students were.

In fact, such a strong sense of belonging to the class seems to be a feature of some of the more provocative attempts to teach rhetorical awareness in recent years. Pamela Annas's (1985) experiments with women's writing classes (in which women see themselves as allies before trying to write to audiences outside the classroom), Shirley Heath's (1983) experiments with student ethnographies (where students see themselves, as a class, as involved in an ongoing research project in their community), and John Rouse's (1985) writing workshops (where students come to see themselves as members in an organization before attempting to write to groups outside the class) are all examples of teaching strategies that allow class membership to develop before the problem of audience is broached. In each of these cases, classroom activities first establish supportive and communal implied identities for students, and only then are students confronted with the conflicts and hostilities of "writing to an audience." In a way, this idea of developing membership in the classroom before teaching audience is merely an extension of our first implication. Developing membership in one's classroom is a way of creating a range of implied identities for students in a class; the general point, of course, is to be aware of what implied identities are created and to think about the ways these implied identities might help or hinder learning.

In conclusion, then, all of our implications (for both teaching and research) stem from a similar perspective. Our study asks teachers and researchers to begin to look at writing and education from a conflict and negotiation perspective. When seen from this perspective, learning to write becomes a problem of identity negotiation within the complex social situation that is the contemporary classroom. Somehow, students will find ways to make their classroom experience support their self-conceptions, their senses of "who they are" in and out of classrooms. Somehow, writing will get mixed up in these negotiations. Our study, in short, suggests that those of us in the field of writing education need to pay more attention to such dynamics of classes and learning, for in these dynamics are the aspects of writing that students will make their own. By studying these dynamics, we may come to understand them; once we understand them, we can use them to teach more effectively.

Appendixes
Works Cited

Appendix 1
Transcript of Interview with Small Group One
(Doug, Susan, George, Kris, Interviewer)
December 1983

Notes on Transcription

In transcribing the spoken interview to printed form, we have observed the following conventions:

1. All spelling has been regularized, even in those cases where actual pronunciation differed from standard written English. "Gonna," for example, is printed as "going to."
2. Nonlinguistic vocal noises like gasps, laughs, and throat clearings have been largely eliminated from the transcription.
3. Overlaps in conversation are marked by large brackets on the right side of the overlapping utterances.
4. Pauses of 2 seconds or more are marked in parentheses.
5. Underlining is used to mark a speaker's emphasis.
6. Dashes are used to represent broken off or unfinished utterances.

The Transcript

Interviewer: What I'm interested in . . . I mean, I've told you before that, that, uh (2 second pause) I'm—you—you know the circumstances, I'm teaching, I'm thinking about using some of the things that Robert's used this quarter as part of my new class next quarter, and I'm interested in a <u>student's</u> point of view. I mean, I've—I've sat in the class with you guys, and I—I know what <u>I</u> saw going on, uh (2 second pause) but I don't know what it felt like to you. So, I'm interested in whatever <u>you</u> have to say about the class. (3 second pause) You know, what—what do you feel like you're going to take from the class if anything? What you felt like Robert's goals were? What you <u>felt</u>. Period. All of that's—anything goes, I really don't, you know, I really don't, uh (2 second pause) have any biases or particular interests. I am just interested in some, some input about this—

George: I like it. <u>Now</u>. But it was really confusing at first, it was really confusing at first, I didn't like it at all. Then, once I, once I saw what he was trying to do and stuff (2 second pause) makes sense. Makes more sense than other teachers who they just concentrate on spelling and stuff like that. He concentrates on what's in your writing not on spelling and stuff like that—audience and stuff like (2.5 second pause) form. (2 second pause) You know, what your writing (2 second pause) what's in it. (2 second pause) That's what I thought he did different from other courses.

Doug: It's— ⎫
George: 'Cause you— ⎬
can use that when you get out of, when you get out of that class, you have to write to a certain audience and stuff, you know how to write to an audience.

(4 second pause)

George: All right, <u>you</u> guys.

Doug: Well I'm (2 second pause) I'm just have to take this 'cause I—I have to take it, you know, it's—I didn't—I, you know, do too well. I <u>understood</u> what he was trying to <u>do</u>, but I thought it was a little <u>vague</u>.

Interviewer: How so?

(2 second pause)

Doug: Like it wasn't <u>explained</u> very well. It, I mean, like examples were given, and that was it, you were supposed to take it from there and know how to do it, you know.

George: And, well—⎱
Doug: I couldn't—   ⎰
I couldn't really—I <u>understood</u> it, but I couldn't do it <u>myself</u> because I just never could solve that, you know, that dimension of it.

George: Yeah, I know what you mean—

(2 second pause)

Doug: Particle-wave-field, you know, I'd try doing that a couple of times, wave tagmemics, and try to follow his example that he gave us for the *Rocky Horror Picture Show.* (2 second pause) It <u>worked</u> a <u>little</u> bit, but I got confused on some of the things. He gave us that diagram on how to <u>do</u> it and I—I didn't know what he was asking, you know.

(3 second pause)

Doug: A little confusing for me, I guess.

(4 second pause)

Interviewer: You know— ⎱
Susan: I—   ⎰
Interviewer: We're going—we're going— ⎱
Susan: [laughs]   ⎰
Interviewer: We're going counterclockwise around your bit—then I get to say my part—

Susan: I thought, like, a lot of it was a waste of time, like the tagmemics, and all—and the particle-wave-field, I—that didn't help me at all. And I <u>think</u>—another thing is he stresses <u>too</u> much on the notebooks. I mean he would be giving me, like, "A"s and "B"s on my papers and a "D" on my notebook 'cause I don't <u>prepare</u> and if I can write a good paper then I don't feel I should have to sit down for four hours, and be writing in my notebook, you know, when I have ideas in my head, I—I just think it through, I don't write it through.

Doug: Yeah, I had to—
Susan: Yeah.   ⎱
Doug: I had to   ⎰
I had to write an <u>essay</u> for another class, and I just read the information I needed to know for that essay, and I wrote down the stuff for the professor, and I got an "A" on the paper. Now, if I would have done that for this class, I probably would have got a "D" on the notebook and a "D" on the paper, you know. I guess if that's two different things that he wants, I guess. I mean, he wants—my <u>other</u> professor wanted—I don't know, I guess I was doing all right with<u>out</u> the stuff. (2 second pause) It's sort of

like what Susan was saying—
Susan: What'd he say, ten pages of tagmemics?
Doug: Yeah.
Susan: I mean, I—I wrote a page and a half, I don't understand how any-body could write ten pages with tagmemics.
George: That's true.
Susan: It was good <u>humor</u>, I couldn't even believe it.
Kris: I—   ⎫
Susan: The ⎭
rushwriting helped.
(2 second pause)
Kris: I don't like—I mean I like—the, like George said, the things that he did were great, working with audience and stuff like that, and, you know, <u>not</u> just working with spelling, but I don't like the way he grades at all, because I think that if you don't do exactly what he had in mind—
George: Uh-hunh.
Kris: that he'll give you a bad grade, and like with—
Doug: Yeah, and you have no way of
knowing—   ⎫
Kris: just this last—   ⎭
with this—with this last assignment, he told me—Okay, I do my pro-posal he didn't like that. So he tells me something else to do. So I do that, and I, you know, he said to, um, explain how Freud would've, or tell what—how Freud would've explained Tess, I <u>did</u> it—<u>that</u>. Exactly what I did. (2 second pause) But I didn't do it in the way <u>he</u> would have done it, and so he gives me a "D"—
Susan: Um-hmm.
Kris: and you know I don't—maybe my—I'm not saying my paper was wonderful, but I don't think it deserved a "D." I mean, a "D" that's very—I mean that's very bad, and I, I mean, maybe, maybe a "B" or a—a "C," I mean, just—
George: I got a "C."
(2 second pause)
Kris: Yeah, see, I don't think you—I don't think that what he gave all of us were really—I mean, I don't think your paper deserved a "C"—
Susan: Well, he gave me an "A," but he wrote my paper. He, he actually— ⎫
Kris: No—   ⎭

he gave you an "A" on the other part, I got an "A" on that part too. He gave you
a "C"—   ⎫
Doug: Yeah— ⎬
as a final—   ⎭
Kris: on the, if you handed that in as a final paper. And I mean I put a lot of work into that too, and you know not (2 second pause) just cause it wasn't what he wanted—
Interviewer: You'll have to explain to me a little bit about the grading because I—that, you know—I've sat in class, and I've sat in on some of your conferences, but I haven't seen any of your papers.
Kris: Okay, well, he gives you two grades, one if you—just for that assignment, it's—you know—
Doug: As it is now— ⎫
Kris: if you did—   ⎬
no—   ⎫
Doug: Go ahead. ⎬
Kris: If you did what you were supposed to, like (2 second pause) you know, we were working with audience, and if you just did it—like if your rough draft <u>was</u> a rough draft, I mean it's <u>that</u> kind of—and then, he gives you a second grade, which is what it'd be if you handed it in as a final paper.
Doug: As it is, yeah.
(3 second pause)
Kris: And it just—it makes me—it really bothers me that—
Interviewer: Why does he do all?
Kris: I don't know.
Doug: So he—   ⎫
George: You know ⎬
where you—
Doug: Just shows us where we're at, right now, I guess.
Kris: Well, 'cause I know—I mean, it's <u>worth</u> it on this paper, on this <u>last</u> paper, to do that, but on all the other papers, we weren't handing it in as a final paper, so it didn't <u>matter</u> what, I mean, unless he was <u>using</u> those grades, I don't know, or something.
(3 second pause)
Interviewer: Hmm.
(5 second pause)

Interviewer: What— ⎫
Susan: Some—   ⎬

like, for one of my papers, he, he told me that he wanted me to get help, so he sent me to the Writing Lab? This is good humor, so um, we— [chuckle]—we were doing a collage and a tree and uh, what was that—

Kris: Outline.

Susan: other one? An <u>outline</u>. So I went to my tutor, and he said "You mean like a picture collage?" He goes "Is that what he's asking you to do? And a family tree?"—Now <u>how</u> can he send me to a <u>tutor</u> and tell me to get help when my tutor had <u>no idea</u>, he said "I've never even <u>heard</u> of a collage, I've never"—you know—"I've never <u>written</u>, done trees." So I—I mean, even <u>they</u> didn't know it, so I then <u>I</u> went to him, and I said "This is really wasting my <u>time</u>, you're the only one that can <u>help</u> me" and he starts in how he's never seen students on a regular <u>basis</u>, and he starts telling me how he wants me to take the class again next <u>quarter</u> and I said "I <u>won't</u>. I absolutely will <u>not</u>," I said "I am doing a <u>very</u> good job in here," so then he says "If you don't want to take the class, that would be a waste for you to take the class." So <u>now</u> ever since then I've been getting excellent grades on my papers, and he—they've been the way he wants to <u>see</u> them, he tells me how to do them, I do them exactly the way he wants them, I'm getting good grades, but that isn't the way I'd write my papers, so I—I'm afraid that I don't know what's going to happen when I get <u>out</u> of the class, 'cause I won't keep writing my papers the way he wants them—

Kris: I mean, his <u>ideas</u> make sense when he tells you, you know, I mean if—when he told me about my paper what was wrong, I mean, it <u>makes</u> <u>sense</u>, but I—

Interviewer: What—

Kris: But that doesn't mean—   ⎫
Interviewer: Give me an example ⎬

you see, I don't exactly know what you're talking about—

Kris: Okay, you mean of what—

Interviewer: Yeah, what you say— ⎫
Kris: he wrote on my paper?   ⎬

Interviewer: What you're talking about, 'cause—

Kris: Okay.

Interviewer: You say that when he gives you an example it makes sense, so it—

Kris: Okay—
Interviewer: explains— ⎱
Kris: He—Okay
when I write my proposal— ⎱
Interviewer: You write what— ⎰
and then he said what.
Kris: Okay—
I wrote my— ⎱
Interviewer: 'Cause I don't see yet— ⎰
Kris: my proposal, on what I was going to do for this academic thing. And
I was going to do, use these books I've read, like *Tess, Madame Bovary*
and *The Plague,* and I was going to, um—Do you remember what I was
going to do? Something with the psychological problems that the people
had in the books. So he thought that it was—he gave me a "D" on that
proposal because he thought that was too broad. So then he tells me, "instead of using all those books take one book and maybe" like he said
"show how Maslow would've talked about Madame Bovary or how Freud
would've explained Tess." So then I did how Freud would've explained
Tess. (2 second pause) Then I hand that in, as my rough draft. Then I get
this thing back—he writes a book on my paper— ⎱
Susan: [laughs]   ⎰
Kris: What looks like a whole piece of paper saying that I didn't get the
audience and that this audience, the literary audience needs this, and
the psychoanalytic audience needs something else, and it wasn't right
and all this stuff. But I mean it makes, you know, (2 second pause) it
made sense that I could, you know, do it in another way that he said. But
he'd already told me to do it this way (2 second pause) and so then telling
me to do it another way, and then if it doesn't say exactly how he thinks it
should be said, I mean if he—if he thinks—if—if—if—maybe it's just
not the way he thinks it should be then he doesn't have to give me an "A"
but just because, you know, doesn't mean that it's worth a "D." That's
what I mean.
(2 second pause)
Interviewer: So, I mean I get the impression from what you're saying,
you know, correct me if I'm wrong, I get the impression from what you're
saying that, that, you—you've all, you've all agreed that there's a certain
amount of vagueness about it, George suggested that, that, uh (2 second
pause) he thought he could see the point after a while, but that it still
bothered him

that—   ⎫
George: Yeah. ⎭

Interviewer: it was vague—is that pretty much what you said?

George: About that.

Interviewer: But you, you guys have also I think said, and you particularly Kris are saying that, that, um, he's vague, but he also had real specific things he wants, and that you

just can't figure them out—   ⎫
Susan: But only he knows what he wants, ⎭

none of us knows.

Kris: See, we're supposed to be—
we're supposed to be learning how to do this, I mean, we've never done this before. And, you know, he can't expect us to—

Doug: [snaps fingers]

pick it up—   ⎫
Kris: You know— ⎭

Doug: Like that.

Kris: You know he can't expect us to know

exactly what he wants—   ⎫
Susan: He should give you ⎭

a lot of credit for trying rather than just knocking it down.

Kris: And also I think that—that's not the only thing he should be grading on,

I mean—   ⎫
Interviewer: What? ⎭

What is?

Kris: Audience. I mean, 'cause that's practically all he, you know, I mean, he, when he writes, this might not make a big difference but when he writes, I mean he can barely even write. His sentences—I mean when he writes things to me, I can barely understand practically what he's saying, you know, he—he can barely even write sentences sometimes. You know, and I think—I mean I don't think that the old is the way he should be grading on, like George said, but I think that it should make some difference if you can, you know, 'cause I said that when I'm writing, I spend a lot of time, I have a lot of problems with switching tenses all the time—I spend a lot of time making sure that I don't. 'Cause with other teachers that's going to make a difference, not only your audience and I don't think that he even looks at that at all.

(2 second pause)

Interviewer: Okay.

Then do— ⎱
Susan: I think— ⎰
audience is going to be <u>obvious</u>, I mean if you're writing a—the only person that has to read it really is your professor, I mean that—it's <u>obvious</u> that you're writing it to him. I don't know why he spent so much time on audience.

Interviewer: But George, <u>you</u> said that you thought it was, there was some <u>point</u> in it.

George: Yeah!

Kris: Well <u>I</u> think there is, you know— ⎱
George: But he said that—then get out of school— ⎰
if you're not going to write for other people, I mean, you know how to evaluate the audience, you know how to write for them,

you know what they want— ⎱
Kris: In your way of— ⎰
I think that's important.

George: You know how to find out what they want and stuff like that. I <u>never</u> did <u>that</u> before.

(2 second pause)

Kris: Well 'cause my dad—I know that's true because my dad's, my dad's um, he writes a, he's an editor of a newspaper and he writes an article for the weekend. He, you know, he just—<u>he has to be</u> aware of who he's writing to, and, I mean it's <u>true</u>. He's <u>not</u> just writing to a teacher, he's writing to, you know, whoever's going to read the paper. So it's—I think, you know, it's important, but—

(2 second pause)

Interviewer: But?

Kris: They should— ⎱
Susan: Well I think ⎰
maybe they should emphasize that on the second level comp class and not the first, and emphasize on the—

Kris: I know, but that— ⎱
Susan: structure and— ⎰

Kris: But people don't take that, not everybody'll take that.

(3 second pause)

Susan: I heard everybody takes that

when— ⎱
Kris: What— ⎰

Susan: you're a junior in college everybody takes that—
Kris: Oh, you have to take <u>that</u>!
Susan: Yeah.
Doug: Um-hmm.
Kris: Oh!   ⎫
Susan: 'Cause   ⎭
then you'll be, I mean, right now as a freshman we're looking at four years of writing to professors, not, you know, eight years from now. (3 second pause)
Doug: When I first started this class I didn't know what to expect from it. (2 second pause) Right now, it seems like it was designed to make us, it was designed for beginning writers who had a writing career ahead of them that they <u>wanted</u> to <u>do</u>, you know. I thought it was like freshman composition, something that'll (3 second pause) I don't know what I expected, but, uh, it's <u>not</u> what he gave, I guess, is what I'm trying to say. I don't think the class was (2.5 second pause) for what it sounded like at first (2 second pause) what it was supposed to be.
Susan: And each class is so different too. (2 second pause)
I mean—   ⎫
Interviewer: What do you   ⎭
mean by that?
Susan: I mean I have, I know other people that are in this year and they're—<u>one</u> of them had to write a <u>paragraph</u> describing a problem, that was their assignment, they're writing <u>poetry</u> I just—it's <u>incredible</u> how much, you know, it varies. (2 second pause) I don't know <u>anybody</u> that's doing <u>this</u>, I mean, I've—I've, you know, people that I live in the dorm and I've asked people to help me and <u>they</u> didn't even understand it. So that's really, 'cause if everybody's doing the same <u>thing</u> at least you could help each other.
(3 second pause)
Interviewer: Have you been able to help each other (2 second pause) as a <u>smaller</u> group? You know, you said that if you live in a dorm you could help each other if everybody was doing the same thing, well has there been some support in the class?
Susan: Not in our group?
Kris: Like—
Susan: Not really because— ⎫
Kris: See, because we—   ⎭
Susan: None of us—

Kris: If, like, if I tell George
what to do—
Doug: Yeah, we're no
experts on the side.
Kris: You know—
Susan: Yeah.
Kris: It doesn't,
it's just the same—
Susan: It's our opinion.
Kris: the same as if George would've thought of it himself, because if
Robert isn't going to like it
I think—
George: Yeah.
Kris: It's good, I mean, you know—
Susan: Robert's got to help—
Kris: Because we can't—
Susan: us—
Kris: Yeah—
Susan: ahead of time—
Kris: I mean when he's there—
Susan: Without a doubt—
Kris: It was much better when he was in our conference group rather
than when we were
just by ourselves—
George: 'Cause he
lets you know what he wants.
Kris: Right. And then—
George: You can tell he's directing the conversation the way he wants
it to go.
Interviewer: Give me an example of that. If you can. If—can you think of
anything in particular?
(3 second pause)
George: I can tell in class when he's putting stuff up on the
board—
Doug: You can tell—
hints stuff, he's trying to
give us the hints somewhat—
George: Yeah, he's trying to hint stuff,
and somebody will put in an idea, and that's not what he wants, and
shoves it aside, and then he gets what he wants down,

like if— ⎱
Kris: Yeah ⎰
'Cause whenever— ⎱
Doug: The—he started directing— ⎰
Kris: He asking us questions— ⎱
Doug: toward a certain goal. ⎰
Kris: He already has the answer in mind,
like if— ⎱
Susan: Yeah, ⎰
it doesn't even pay— ⎱
George: He does. You've got to call— ⎰
Susan: to raise your hand 'cause he writes down your answer and then
two minutes later it's "Ah. Wrong." You know.
(2 second pause)
Kris: Well I mean, you know, that's okay if, you know, someone says the
wrong answer, but it's with the—and you know it's just like everything,
it's like that, you know, he always has,
you know— ⎱
Doug: What— ⎰
Kris: one way of—
George: One way of doing it—
Kris: Um-hmm.
(2 second pause)
Interviewer: So do— ⎱
George: It's true. ⎰
(4 second pause)
George: I still think it's a good course.
Interviewer: Why?
Kris: Well I think it <u>is</u> but I think—
George: It's helping me. I can tell. I'm working hard.
Interviewer: 'Cause you're working hard. You know somebody that's—
George: I feel like I'm making progress.
Interviewer: In what direction?
George: Audience and stuff like that.
(2 second pause)
Kris: But then— ⎱
George: My first ⎰
papers were just (3 second pause) <u>bad</u>, (2 second pause) but then as I got
more—I suppose if he would've <u>said</u> what he wanted I could've done it

faster—but he doesn't really tell you what he wants, he just says "Write to an audience."

Interviewer: If he'd said what he wanted, what do you think he would have said? You guys all seem to be suggesting that he's got real specific wants that—that you (2 second pause) what? Try to figure out or—

George: Yeah.   }
Interviewer: try to—   }

satisfy, okay? I mean, can you tell me what they are?

(2 second pause)

Interviewer: Or is it still pretty—   }
George: What he wants?   }

Interviewer: mysterious?

Doug: Well—the audience, he wants us to write to a specific audience and make it a real small audience (2 second pause) or like, the tag-memics, he wants the notebook, he—we have to do lots of preparatory work that's 67 percent of our grade.

(2 second pause)

Kris: What—   }
Susan: And—   }

Kris: What he—   }
Susan: Just outrageous. }

Kris: What he did, okay, for one of the assignments, I think it was the second exercise, I did something to it with the telephone and then he told, you know, he said I had to make my audience more specific. So then I revised it once, and then he said that it was more clear, but, you know, he was kind of like hinting around you know but maybe these people don't have a big attention span and they'd want it not enclosed but maybe in another way, so he, you know, he was like telling me how he, how he thought it should be and then, only then, would it be right, you know, and so I did it again and I put little topic headings and stuff like that, but that—and you know I knew that's what he wanted. (2 second pause) So that's what I did. For him, you know, to hand in Wednesday.

(2 second pause)

George: So—what's for Wednesday?

Kris: Well, it's that—you know how you—you already handed yours in, your collage, you know, that you revised?

(2 second pause)

George: You haven't handed yours in yet?

Kris: No.

George: Oh, is that what you're doing for?

(2 second pause)

Kris: Yes. I already did it.

(2 second pause)

Interviewer: Hmm.

George: That's about it.

Kris: Um-hmm.

Interviewer: What do you—what do you think the general reaction of the class is to the class—is you guys—

are you—are your responses— ⎫
Susan: They really—   ⎭

frustration.

Kris: It is. Very frustrated. Very—

George: Nobody knows what's going on.

Susan: I know a lot of people in there, like, live in the dorms and they're just like,

shaking their heads all the time. ⎫
Kris: Yeah, you can't—   ⎭

you can't figure out, you know, I mean, then you think you do it right, and then you get a "D," and then you'll have—

George: It's not like math or anything, where you know you have problems, you—

Doug: Right.

George: do it this way, and that's the way there is to

do it.   ⎫
Kris: Um-hmm. ⎭

(2 second pause)

Kris: And also— ⎫
George: And so I ⎭

back and forth, I mean a lot of—

Interviewer: Is that part of the nature of the class or is that just part of the nature of the subject?

(2 second pause)

Doug: I think it's the nature of the subject.

George: Subject, but it's his, moreso here—

Kris: I know, but you'd think you'd get good at it, 'cause like last year when I had my AP English class you know, the first paper was real hard to write 'cause you didn't know how to do it, you know, and at least the teacher expected the same sort of thing each time, but it seems like each

time with <u>him</u> you got to—you don't have a—it doesn't get
any easier— ⎫
George: Something different— ⎭
Kris: Really!
George: It's something different each time,
you have to be— ⎫
Kris: It doesn't ⎭
really get any easier, and you figure, and if you're making an outline (2
second pause) for your own self, I mean, you're not going to worry about
"well, wait, what's my audience? Are they, is this right for them?" You
know if you're making an outline just for yourself you're not, that just
doesn't seem important, but, you know, when he had us make that outline, I don't see what the purpose of that was.
(2 second pause)
Kris: I mean, it had to be so specific and so perfect.
Interviewer: Um.
(5 second pause)
Interviewer: Hm.
(6 second pause)
Interviewer: Well, what would you tell me if I were going to take something from this class to use in a class next quarter, what would I—what
should I use and what should I change?
(2 second pause)
George: I don't know.
Interviewer: What would you keep and what would you throw out?
(3 second pause)
Doug: Well you could keep <u>everything</u>, I think, but it's just—
Susan: I would, um— ⎫
Kris: (word garbled) ⎭
it d'fferently.
Susan: Yeah, like—
Doug: Do it
differently— ⎫
Susan: Let them ⎭
know how to do these things, but—tagmemics and the rushwriting, you
know, those things—
Kris: And don't make them do it— ⎫
Susan: But let them— ⎭

Doug: Just don't— ⎱
Susan: Let them ⎰
decide which way is best for them.

Kris: And don't make them, you know, like in our notebooks, he said that what we were missing the first time? We had to <u>do</u> for now, I mean we had to go back and do those things that you know were from way before, like the purpose defining matrix, I didn't do that the first time, and he <u>never</u> said, I mean I remember when he you know handed it, that thing, out, the sheet with it on—he didn't say "now, <u>do</u> this and make sure it's in your notebook" he just said—

George: Yeah.

Kris: You know, "go home and maybe read through this, answer the questions." <u>I</u> had no idea that he wanted it in the notebook, so then I had to sit there, couple weeks ago one night, and just do it, it took, you know, like a half an hour to sit there and do it, and it didn't—I did it for something that was a long time ago and it had no purpose (3 second pause) at all.

(6 second pause)

Kris: So don't, don't <u>make</u> them do things that don't help them.

Interviewer: Okay—what else?

(2 second pause)

Kris: Well just, you know, tell them about rushwriting and about those things, and if they, you know, they can try it, but they don't have to use it, you know, they don't have to have a big notebook that doesn't mean that they're doing better than if they have a small notebook.

(2 second pause)

Interviewer: Okay.

George: Specify what you want of them.

Interviewer: What do you mean? ⎱
Doug: Make clear—   ⎰

George: So—so—okay, "I want this in your notebook," that, you know, "you can do this" or "I want a draft." Tell them exactly what you want, "I want <u>this</u> in your notebook, I want <u>that</u>, I want that, I want that." (3 second pause) Then they'll <u>do</u> it.

(5 second pause)

Kris: And it could be more like a journal where, you know, they could <u>write</u> in there, "Well I didn't do it because it didn't help me when I tried it or something," you know. They don't have to just sit there and do it because they're supposed to, 'cause they have to.

Interviewer: Okay.

(2 second pause)

Interviewer: So that's a change you'd make.

(2 second pause)

George: Well— ⎱
Doug: With   ⎰
all these things that he, all those topics like tagmemics and audience and all that other stuff, I think it's too much to try and put in one quarter.

Quite a task—   ⎱
Kris: Yeah, I didn't ⎰
don't even know what tagmemics was supposed to do. I mean how I—

Doug: Like we—we spent like a week on each topic, which you could have spent like two or three weeks on, you know? It's—

Interviewer: Give me an example of that.

Doug: Well, well I've said like earlier, tagmemics, he gave us (2 second pause) thing on *Rocky Horror Show* about four pages long, "This is how I did it. Did it last night and—"That was it, you know, "Here it is. Look at it. You know how to do it from that," you know—

George: Yeah.

(2 second pause)

Susan: Like I can't even—   ⎱
Doug: It's probably ridiculous— ⎰

Susan: understand this. And what were those other things he passed out, on Darwin and all those things? I didn't, that was so, such a waste of time to me—   ⎱
Doug: Yeah. Those collages— ⎰

Susan: I didn't understand any of it.

(2 second pause)

Doug: He gives us examples. "Here it is. Learn it. Do it."

Susan: And like what was he lecturing about the other day? I didn't remember at all—

Kris: Oh yeah.

Susan: Friday.

It must have been Friday.   ⎱
Kris: Must have been then— ⎰

Susan: For the whole hour he stood up there and talked, and I, I didn't even—

Interviewer: What was he talking about?

Doug: About revising

your paper—
Kris: How to revise—
how, uh—
Doug: How a pro writer
would revise—
Kris: Would do it—
you know the—when they revise, they just look at their sentences and take it so far as, maybe change a word here or there, but, uh—which is obvious I mean we know that, but we're not professional writers who, you know, who are going to—
Susan: And he was telling us—
Doug: Look at our own, that uh—
Kris: I mean, that—
that we are freshmen, that's how we do
do it—
Susan: He was
telling us, he was showing us grades that he had gotten and "D"s that he had gotten and how tough his professors were
on him and—
Kris: Like, you know,
it's why he's tough on us—
Susan: I think that's why he—
you know,
he figures—
Kris: He likes
to do it too [chuckles].
Susan: He had it.
(4 second pause)
Kris: I think he—I mean, he likes to be—he always picks everything apart. Too much, I think, I mean it—no, not—think he should just "Oh, this is okay, I'll give it an 'A'" but—
Susan: Be easier.
Kris: He just, I mean 'cause it's so frustrating, I mean I'm not, you know it's, if you deserve the grades, then you get it but it shouldn't—so—frustrates, you know, work so hard, and, you know—
Doug: Yeah.
Kris: And do what you think he wants, and then have it not be that, and get a "D" and have it be totally wrong and have to totally re-do it.
(2 second pause)

Doug: Yeah, you write the paper and you think you covered all the points, and then you get the paper back and he says "Nope. Didn't get it at all. Try again."

Kris: 'Cause I don't
think revising—
Doug: That's all you get. }

Kris: should be re-doing everything 'cause that's what I had to do, I mean I had to write a whole new paper, just <u>revising</u>.

Interviewer: Um-hmm. What do you think revising <u>should</u> be? Just—

Kris: Um, <u>changing</u> what you already, you know, change—I mean, it could be a lot of changes, but (3.5 second pause) I mean, I think like (2 second pause) with—how I normally write is I write a rough draft, and then, then when I just <u>recopy</u> it, that's when I revise, you know when I— rewriting it over, then I just change, you know, switch things around maybe switch paragraphs around or—

Doug: [chuckles] It's just— }
Kris: Yeah, }

put in a new word here or there, or a, um (5 second pause), you know, things like that.

Interviewer: Um-hmm.

Kris: Put in more.

Interviewer: Um-hmm.

Kris: Cut out things.

(2 second pause)

Interviewer: Well, well, okay so I've got some—well, at least as—this— this—sounds like evaluation's a problem, and it sounds like, uh (2 second pause) the expectations for the notebook need to be redefined from <u>your</u> point of view. What, if—what, if anything, would you <u>keep</u>? What <u>wouldn't</u> you change?

(2 second pause)

Doug: Audience,
that's— }
George: Audience, }
yep.

Doug: You know, that's—

(2 second pause)

Interviewer: What about it?

Doug: Writing for a specific audience—

George: It's good for you.

Doug: Yeah, it helps you, uh (2.5 second pause) it helps you meet your reader's needs, part of, and you, you can write what they want, and it helps you to better <u>understand</u> what, what they want also, I guess.

Kris: I think also maybe more specific subjects, I mean when he says, you know, every single thing you could write on just <u>anything</u>, and when you have to, you know, pick <u>any</u> subject and then you have to narrow that down, and pick an audience out of that and then do <u>all</u> that, I mean it takes you—because you think, you know, you have an <u>idea</u>, and then that's too broad, and then you have to keep, you know, making it more specific and stuff.

(2 second pause)

Interviewer: So you'd say that was a negative—

Kris: Yeah.

(2 second pause)

Interviewer: Okay. Is that a general feeling?

(2 second pause)

George: I'd say.

Doug: Yeah, I'd say.

(2 second pause)

Interviewer: Okay. You guys—Susan, you mentioned that, that you had heard other people talking about their comp classes and none of them were like this. Um (3.5 second pause) what's—what's your reaction to that? I mean, what's (3 second pause) how does this compare to those, in your opinion?

Susan: It <u>doesn't</u>. I mean, theirs is just—I mean maybe theirs is too easy, but I think ours is too hard. I really do.

(2 second pause)

Interviewer: What do—what do you mean too easy?

Whereas—   ⎫

Susan: Well— ⎬

writing poetry! That's really not something you're going to be doing in college, you know—

Interviewer: Uh-hunh.

Susan: And little papers, but, I think—like, he doesn't go into research papers at all, Robert, and I think that's important, I think we're going to be doing a lot of those and I'd like to learn how to do them better—you too? That's something, you know, that I—rather than last minute and then, when our final paper, I thought "Oh good, we're finally going to do a <u>research</u> paper," he says "This is <u>not</u> a <u>research</u> paper" so there we go, you know—

Doug: And lots of help.

Susan: I think we're—we should have to learn what, you know, to look things up and put a lot of—I think we should be putting our time into that rather than sitting down and rushwriting or sitting down and, you know, digging out facts.

(4 second pause)

Interviewer: So, that's a consensus too?

George: Yeah. (2 second pause) You know he never, he never got into footnoting or anything like that, he didn't say anything about it—

Susan: Nope.

George: I don't know if I need to footnote this last paper or not.

Kris: I didn't. And also you know with like, with Susan he'd color, you know, he took her last paper and he marked all the spelling and sentence mistakes—

Susan: He said that
was the only thing wrong—
Kris: He totally marked them.

But he didn't, but he didn't tell her how to, he didn't, I mean, he just marked them, he doesn't, I don't even think he graded you on that, you know—

Susan: He just said that—

Kris: He just—

Susan: Organization was excellent, and, and content was excellent, and then says you have to work on splinters, and he underlined whenever I violated—
Kris: Yeah, but see he

doesn't, you know, I mean he, he just, you know, that was just something marked in it, you know he had all these blue lines and he didn't, you know when you went to your, your little meetings with him did he help you on that or anything? I mean (3.5 second pause) I don't know. I mean 'cause she had done the other things, I mean she did the audience and she did, but—

(2 second pause)

Susan: I think he, like, grades on whatever he can find wrong at the time. [laughs] You know, he gives—on mine, he—the audience was great and the content and then the—because the spelling he gave me an "A/C." So—

(8 second pause)

Interviewer: Okay. Well, is there anything else I need to know?

Kris: [chuckles] Now that we totally cut him down [laughs] um (2 second pause) or, uh, I did.

Doug: Really?

Kris: Um-hmm.

George: I saw good points in the course.

Interviewer: You did? What?

George: Well, audience stuff and then the—

Kris: You like— ⎫
Susan: You said ⎭

that already ten times. ⎫
Kris: Yeah, you, you ⎭

liked it so you say what's good about it, because I didn't like it [chuckles]. (3 second pause)

George: I still think his discussions are structured to go on a certain way, each discussion I mean I could tell—

Doug: [laughs]

George: I would—I'd say something, I'd say something, you know, I— "Hey, I got a good idea, I'll say it." He puts it up. Then two seconds later he'd ask some question to lead somebody to say something else, would put a whole new different idea up on the board that you could just tell he was moving it this way (2 second pause) with all the answers—I don't know. That's what I don't like.

You know if it's just discussions— ⎫
Susan: If he knew his answers, ⎭

he should have put up

his answers— ⎫
George: Why is he even bothering ⎭

to have discussions— ⎫
Susan: And not even asked us. ⎭

Kris: And you know what else?

George: When he knows what it's going to be?

Kris: That one day when he had Doug go up there and do his whole thing? What was the purpose for the rest of us, just sitting there?

Doug: Yeah, I know—

Kris: For forty-five minutes. ⎫
Doug: I was—I was ⎭

wasting all your guy's time.

Susan: I couldn't believe it—

Kris: I mean, it wasn't your fault, but—

Doug: I didn't even <u>use</u> that— ⎫
Susan: We spent a whole hour— ⎭
Kris: What was the point in that—
Susan: on helping him.
Kris: You know, why did we— ⎫
Doug: I didn't even use that. ⎭
Kris: need to be there? You know—
Susan: <u>He</u> should have gotten together with Doug and <u>he</u> should have helped Doug—
Doug: <u>Yeah.</u> ⎫
Kris: Okay— ⎭
Susan: Because he knew what he, you know— ⎫
Doug: On a one-to-one basis— ⎭
Kris: I mean—what was the point of being there, you know—
Doug: I wasted a whole hour of your guy's time.
(2 second pause)
George: Yeah, you <u>did</u>, didn't you?
Kris: Of course—yeah, you know— ⎫
Interviewer: [laughs] ⎭
Kris: How true!
Doug: It was—it wasn't up to me.
Kris: Yeah, it wasn't your fault, I mean—
Susan: And he was still lost at the end of the hour.
(2 second pause)
George: I know.
I didn't see why really— ⎫
Kris: Any you know, ⎭
everybody else in the class is going to have, you know, they'll have ideas, but <u>still</u>, so they—we're supposed to give Doug ideas, but when we use our ideas on our own papers we get "D"s, so I don't understand—
Doug: Yeah, how's that— ⎫
Kris: How's ⎭
that supposed to work out, you know, how are we supposed to be able (3 second pause) you know, which I think is <u>good</u> though, I <u>like</u> the conference groups and stuff I mean we should help each other but it, it should really help. He should make it
that it helps. ⎫
Susan: I think in-class ⎭
conferences are of no help because he <u>never</u> gets around to every—you

know, everybody.

George: Yeah.

(3 second pause)

Interviewer: Hmm.

(2 second pause)

Interviewer: Okay.

Susan: We should have stuck with the conferences over at the—

Doug: Then he asks, "is everybody happy?" or uh, "is everyone satisfied?" ⎫
Kris: What ⎭

are we supposed to say?

Doug: Yeah!

Susan: Really! ⎫
Kris: No! ⎭

I suppose saying if I hate this class [laughs].

Doug: Well— ⎫
Kris: You ⎭

bug me, I mean he just makes me mad.

Interviewer: [laughs] ⎫
Kris: You know. ⎭

Susan: He's too set in his ways.

(4 second pause)

Interviewer: What do you mean by that?

Susan: Well he—he knows exactly what he wants to see, and if he doesn't see it, he's like a little kid and you're

the one that suffers— ⎫
Kris: But some professors ⎭

are going to be like that, you have to do what they want, I mean I, [garbled name] told us all about that, I mean, she said with some professors, you could write tons to support your ideas and that kind of stuff, okay but, you know, some other professors are going to say, you know, "This is it, and this is how it goes, and use that thing," and you have to use that, you know, if you write a paper. Well, he didn't say that, you know, he didn't, he didn't give you any idea that you had to do it his way.

(3 second pause)

Kris: He didn't— ⎫
Doug: Gave us— ⎬
Interviewer: Could you— ⎭

Doug: some help. ⎫
Kris: Yeah. ⎭

Doug: Okay.

(4 second pause)

Interviewer: [To George] You still are not persuaded that (3 second pause) their (2 second pause) basically negative point of view is one you should share? [To Kris] Am I right in saying that it—

Kris: Yep.

George: Well, I still, I still think it helped me, the class helped me so why share in the negative view? ⎫
Susan: Well it helped me too, ⎭
but I—it didn't help me as much as I—it should have. There was a lot of things that—that I needed help out of him.

Interviewer: Like what? That you didn't get help on? That is like—

Susan: Like the research papers and the—

Interviewer: Okay.

Kris: 'Cause like he— ⎫
Susan: The [word garbled] you know I— ⎭

Kris: Every single paper was centered on audience. I mean—

Susan: If everyone— ⎫
Kris: It didn't seem, ⎭
it wouldn't seem like it was going to be, but then in the end, that was what it was centered on, you know, even this last paper, you know, supposed to be where you, you know, do a little research and—

Susan: Yeah.

Kris: you know make it sort of—but really the whole thing, I mean, the basic thing was audience again. You know, he could have done that a little bit and then, I mean, worked with, worked a little bit with sentences and writing and, and then maybe done (2 second pause) you know worked with other things too. Maybe just had one week where you go through rushwriting, just practice all those—where you did all those things, and wrote little paragraphs, and little things, and then just—after that one week, use whatever you thought helped you.

Doug: Um-hmm.

Kris: You know, and not the whole, not (2 second pause) you know audience.

(5 second pause)

Interviewer: So you think that the focus on audience is—

(2 second pause)

Susan: It should be brought up, ⎫
but it— ⎭
Interviewer: extreme?

Susan: should not be (2 second pause) in that great a detail—
Kris: [chuckles]
Susan: Gone over that much. I, like—
Interviewer: And George is—
Kris: George disagrees with us— ⎫
Interviewer: <u>smiling</u> because he doesn't really agree, ⎬
is that— ⎭
Susan: Maybe we should have spent
<u>the whole three months</u> on— ⎫
Kris: Well, let George have ⎭
another whole two quarters with Robert, and we'll all [laughs]
George: [chuckles] All right.
Doug: No, I think George just understood it better than us, and was able
to <u>apply</u> it better, like, I draw—
Kris: Then you know— ⎫
Doug: <u>lots</u> of ⎭
mental blanks, and then
I'm— ⎫
Kris: You ⎭
didn't get frustrated, and that's good, but I did.
Susan: I did.
(2 second pause)
Interviewer: You didn't get frustrated?
George: You just got to understand Robert.
Like— ⎫
Kris: I <u>know</u>, ⎭
but I don't think that we—
Interviewer: How so? What do you mean? Just—
George: I don't know. I just understand what he wants.
Susan: Yeah. I understand, he—
we got together— ⎫
George: I can understand ⎭
what he wants.
Susan: on a one-to-one basis, and he told me what to do and he told me
how to do it and I did it and that was, that's
fine. ⎫
George: Write— ⎭
write whatever makes him happy.
Interviewer: What—what—what makes him happy? ⎫
Kris: I don't complain about ⎭

when he helps you write it—⎤
Susan: Yeah, what makes— ⎬
Interviewer: I mean you say ⎦
"you got to understand him"
and it—   ⎤
Kris: So what— ⎦
Interviewer: It sounds like the reason you're not frustrated is because you
do. What, what, what do you understand about Robert that they don't?
Kris: [laughs] God! Has he really spoken to you, or what?
George: What I understand, you got to—
Kris: [laughs] Do you know him? ⎤
George: [laughs]   ⎦
Susan: Personally?
George: You just got to act like—act enthused, got to write, write stuff
enthusiastically, don't get all uptight.
'Cause I was really—   ⎤
Doug: Like you got to— ⎦
George: I was getting—   ⎤
Doug: keep the right attitude, eh? ⎦
George: I was really pissed three weeks into the class, or four weeks—
after our notebook, then I went in and talked to him. I could see what he
wanted and stuff, so I started doing that. Then once you do what, once
you do what he wants, then it's easy because you don't get mad 'cause you
don't get bad grades.
Kris: Yeah, but— ⎤
George: It's—   ⎦
Kris: But other—   ⎤
Doug: It's hard to— ⎦
Kris: Other teachers aren't going to want what Robert wants, so
we should—   ⎤
George: Well that's ⎦
the whole thing! You, that's kind of what's good about this class, you, he's
different, so you got to figure out what he wants, so
other teachers—   ⎤
Kris: I know, but— ⎦
George: You'll be able to figure out what they want.
Kris: Yeah, but other teachers—So what're we going to—what're we sup-
posed to do, get you know totally so that we know what Robert wants,
and then every paper we write it's going to be, oh my god, you're writing
for Robert, you know, you're writing for what Robert wants. Then you

get to another teacher and you're going to be writing that way, if that's not what they want, you don't have—
Susan: And if the teacher says— ⎤
Kris: If it's not a comp class— ⎦
Susan: "You do it the way you want to do it," then how are you, you know, how are you going to know if we been doing it right, because he's so—
Kris: I know, but, you know, other classes maybe you only have to write one paper, so you're just going to have to do it however, you know, and Robert is just trying to teach us to write, you know, his way, but maybe other teachers aren't going to like that so you should just—he should help you figure out what you want to write (2 second pause) but—
George: You kind of put, you write your way, but you still put his ideas, you know, his—
Kris: But he doesn't,
but he, even when— ⎤
Susan: You know, I wouldn't— ⎦
Kris: He's— ⎤
Susan: organize ⎦
the way he organizes.
Kris: He's, to me, he's trying to tell me ⎤
how to write my paper. That's what he's been doing, you know, telling me to do it this way and then he turns out to be more specific, and do it this way, so I just hand them in—
Doug: I don't think it's his way as much as it's the way it should be done.
George: Yeah—
Doug: That's what he's trying to get through.
Susan: Well anyway
we were trying— ⎤
Interviewer: What do you mean by that— ⎦
Susan: He was trying to teach us—
Interviewer: What do you mean by that, Doug?
Doug: I mean that it's not his personal view, it's how he thinks, it's how he interprets what the right way of writing should be done, instead of, it's not something that it's his personal view, it's how, you know, it should be done instead of—
(3 second pause)
Doug: I don't know if you know or not, but [chuckles]
Interviewer: Well, I think I understand what you mean.
(3 second pause)

Interviewer: So—yeah, I—I remember at the beginning of the class, the first couple of weeks when I started sitting in, you [to George] were pretty vocal.

Kris: You were always like— ⎫
George: Un-hunh.   ⎭

Kris: "I don't get it!" [chuckles]

George: [laughs]

Doug: "What do you want?"

Interviewer: And then, and then all of a sudden you got it.

George: I know.

Interviewer: What did you get?

Kris: Yeah. What did you get?

George: I just understood what he wanted.

Susan: Isn't it something that the whole class
forgot—   ⎫
Doug: I think ⎭
he started getting it, all this changed, I was amazed.

George: Yeah. Right. That went on.

Kris: I think you're practically the only one.

George: What?

Kris: Who got it.

Doug: [laughs]

Interviewer: I guess—

Doug: Well, that's—that sounds—   ⎫
Interviewer: What I'm trying to find out ⎭
is what "it" is.

George: Just understand what he, I just understood Robert, you know, I just understood what he wanted then he would say it, you know he's not, he doesn't say some things, but I can understand when he says, mentions something then it's probably important.

Doug: Oh.

George: You know, mentions the notebook, it's important. He mentions it, it's probably important.

Interviewer: I see.

George: So then I, what he mentioned, I put into my writing, or I tried to put that into my writing—

Interviewer: Uh-hunh.

(2 second pause)

Doug: That's very subtle about it, that's—

George: Yeah.

Susan: Well then like I went to
one of the labs— ⎱
Doug: Didn't stress it. ⎰
Susan: you know, one of the labs, and, the—one of the ladies that was teaching, and she helped me, and she gave me a bunch of ideas, and I think they were good ideas, so I put them in my paper, and he just tore them down like "Where did you come up with this information?" [chuckles] Like this's I couldn't even believe it— ⎱
Kris: Oh my gosh! ⎰
Susan: So why does he even tell us to go if he doesn't like what they say? Maybe he should be teaching labs then he'll, then look back.
George: Probably is. Is he?
Kris: I don't know.
Interviewer: I think he did last year, I don't know that he is this year.
George: Is he working for his doctorate?
Interviewer: Yup. He's in the midst of writing his dissertation.
George: So he's just about a professor, huh?
Susan: God help us all.
George: [to Susan and Kris] See!
Kris: Hanhh!
(2 second pause)
Interviewer: "See!" What do you mean,
"See!"? ⎱
George: He probably knows how— ⎰
he probably knows how to write more than you do.
Doug: Yeah, of course he does— ⎱
Susan: Yeah, but he knows how ⎰
to write the way he wants to write, but the way he was taught to write—
George: [to interviewer] What do you think of him as a writer? ⎱
Susan: I was not taught to write that way. ⎰
Kris: He—he's teaching us—
Interviewer: What do I think of him as a writer?
George: Yeah.
Interviewer: Well, I— ⎱
Susan: [chuckles] ⎰
Interviewer: I've read some of his finished work, and I think that it's extremely lucid, very insightful, um (2.5 second pause) he's a very—
George: Hunh!
Interviewer: able writer, I think. For audiences like me.
(3 second pause)

George: For audiences like the other <u>college</u> people?

Interviewer: Yeah. I mean, I would be, I would be an academic audience, and the writing that I've seen of his for that audience. I've seen, for example I'm in a conference group with Robert (2.5 second pause) that we discuss people's dissertation chapters and so forth, so I've seen a number of the chapters from Robert's dissertation.

George: What is a dissertation, a <u>book</u>?

Interviewer: Basically.

George: On how to <u>write</u>, or what?

Interviewer: Uh (2 second pause) Ph.D. dissertations are concentrated in-depth studies, uh, in specific areas of interest. It's a way to demonstrate academically that you have control of a subject in depth, and Robert's is on, uh, composition <u>theory</u>, theories of how people, uh, produce written discourse.

(2 second pause)

George: Is he using the ideas in his dissertation on us?

Interviewer: Uh, I think that, that, <u>I</u> see, from what I've read of his stuff, <u>yes</u> that there are, that, that, some of the research that he's done informs the, the strategies that he's using in your class, yes.

(5 second pause)

George: [To women] See.

Interviewer: What's that mean?

George: I don't know, just—

he's— ⎫
Kris: I'm not ⎭

saying that what he's teaching is bad. At all.

I mean I— ⎫
George: Just the ⎭

way he's doing it?

Kris: Yeah.

Susan: Yeah.

Interviewer: And your basic objection is, that it's—what?

Susan: It's too—

George: Too vague.

Susan: Too—that isn't what to write, it's too—you don't know what he wants.

(2 second pause)

Susan: And he's the only, I mean he <u>sends</u> you to places like the <u>labs</u> and the <u>tutors</u> and they, and <u>they</u> don't help because only he knows what he <u>wants</u>, and the conference groups, you know.

(2 second pause)

Interviewer: Is that a general feeling?

Kris: Umm? ⎫
Doug: Probably. ⎭

(3 second pause)

Interviewer: Okay. Well this is—are—are we done? It's about time. I really appreciate your conversation. Thank you, and—and— ⎫
George: Sure. ⎭

Interviewer: I think I—I want to go back and listen to the conversation over I'm sure there'll be some rich stuff—

George: [laughs] ⎫
Doug: I don't know ⎭

if it'll help you much.

Interviewer: Well, I think that it will, I think that it will.

Doug: 'Cause we are—we're pretty vague ourselves.

Kris: [laughs] ⎫
Interviewer: [laughs] ⎭

George: We're pretty vague too. [laughs]

Kris: [laughs]

(2 second pause)

Interviewer: So the—endemic vagueness going around.

George: Yeah—learning how to be vague.

Kris: [laughs] Yeah that's, that's what the class is [tape ends].

Appendix 2
Full Class Interview
December 1983

Notes on Transcription

Due to a recorder malfunction, the sound quality of the tape of this interview was quite poor. Consequently, the transcription of the interview could not be as accurate as that of the tape in appendix 1. Tape noise made it impossible to hear some speakers, made overlaps in conversation near impossible to untangle, and made calculation of gaps between speakers difficult. The transcription will consequently follow these conventions:

1. Pronunciation and syntax have been largely regularized. Dashes and commas are used to mark breaks in speaking as they are normally used in written English.
2. The symbol (pause) marks an extended break between speakers.
3. Overlaps between speakers are not marked in the text.
4. Underlining is used to mark a speaker's emphasis.

In short, unlike appendix 1, this appendix records only *what* the speakers said without recording *how* it was said. The transcript should not be used for conversational analysis, though it does provide a fuller sense of the range of student response to the course we studied.

The Transcript

Interviewer: Um, you've seen me sitting in here probably for the entire quarter, some of you have noticed me and some of you haven't probably—
[General laughter]
Interviewer: Um, like the good news is you've all been aware that I was here, um, and, I—I should explain to you what I've been doing. Um, some of you know, or have been told, that I have been doing research for my own class. I am an instructor at the University in the comp program. Um, and I have been teaching—and have been interested in this class, um, for my own purposes. But I've also been doing some research on this class as a class. Um, you may or may not be aware that, that the University composition curriculum has been changed dramatically in the last couple of years—you know that? Yes? No? There used to be a two quarter requirement that's in the freshman year only. In other words you would have taken another course this year in sequence after this one in the old days. Um, <u>now</u> you will take this course, and then you'll be required to take another course in your junior or senior year that'll be explicitly related to your major field. So that you'll get specialized training with reference to the kind of real world writing that you'll be expected to do. We, in the process of changing the curriculum, are—have also been involved with <u>evaluating</u> it, with, you know, saying what's working, what isn't working, and I've been sitting in on this class in an effort to study what's going on in this class particularly as kind of a model for other classes. Okay? To sort of get a sense of what's working with reference to <u>Robert's</u> specific curriculum and what's not. Now I've had a chance to talk to some of you, I've sat in on a couple of, a couple of groups, conference groups, and had a chance to talk about the class with some of you. What I'd like to do today for about a half an hour is to get just some general discussion, um, about <u>your</u> sense of what happened in the class. This is your opportunity to—to shape potentially the, the composition program at the University, if you want to think of it that way. Your chance to, to communicate <u>your</u> sense of what the <u>goals</u> in this class were, your sense of your <u>response</u> to the goals, your response to the class in general, how you felt about it. Anything goes. Most of you've heard this spiel before, or some of you have heard this spiel before—anything goes. I'm interested in anything you have to say about the class. Um, none of this will be available to Robert. Um—
[General laughter]

Interviewer: Well, I mean, there may come a point sometime long after when he, you know, he may get a, a look at some of the results of this, um, but, but what goes on in class today will be mine until <u>well after</u> you have your grades, so you don't have to worry about anything like that. I'm really interested in, in whatever you have to say, and anything goes.

(pause)

Interviewer: Just, just jump right in.

Allen: All right. First off, what I thought was you put—right at the beginning of the quarter he said "Well, some people just sit down," there's different ways of writing processes that he said "Well some people just sit down and they can write their final draft right away without any revisions and that's okay." I'm one of those people that does that, and I got marked down because I didn't do my revisions the way he wanted them to do. And he in the beginning said "it's okay." So I think his grading process is totally obscure.

[General class noise]

Allen: Because he was not grading our writing at all, he was grading our process. It didn't matter how good a writer we were as long as we did it <u>his</u> way.

(pause)

Interviewer: Is that a general consensus?

Unidentified female student: Like with our notebooks he put—'cause our notebook, if our notebook's really good he doesn't care what the papers look like, so that's another—

[*Inaudible:* At least three students at once]

Allen: I mean, if we're out, if we're out in real life, how many, how many, if we're handing in a paper for work, how many people are going to say, "Well, you <u>revise</u> it five times, <u>okay!</u>"

[General laughter]

(pause)

Allen: I mean, they're not going to be look—they're going to be looking at our final paper, what <u>that</u> looks like, they're not going to be, you know, "Well. You did, uh, particle wave field here" you know—

[General laughter]

Allen: You know. "He's going to get a, an A for the paper" you know. It's—<u>that's</u> not how it's going to be. He—he just totally graded <u>I</u> think which was totally wrong. The way he graded, he graded on process not our writing.

(long pause)

Interviewer: Anybody feel differently about that?

Kris: Come on, George.

[laughter]

Interviewer: That's a unanimous opinion?

George: No.

[General laughter]

George: I think he was just trying, just trying to shape our writing process by having us do all that stuff. That's what the course was about, he wasn't—okay, maybe at the beginning he said that's how you write, but he wanted to change the way you writed—wrote.

[General laughter]

George: And so that's why he graded all that stuff, I mean, he wasn't really concentrating on the papers but on the process. That's why—

Allen: But if we could—All I'm saying if we could get something, I was getting "A"s on all, every single paper I turned in, but then I got a "C"—

Interviewer: Did you?

Allen: Yeah, but then I got a "C+" on my notebook because I didn't do the process the way he wanted it done. And I don't think—if my writing is that good that I can get "A"s, I should be getting "A"s on my notebook.

(pause)

Carol: I think he was meaning—a problem that the class was more, uh, for people who are having problems with their writing and for people who need to get taught notebooks, and that maybe he kind of like, if it was fine, then he thought it was great, but he also wanted to see that you do a lot of work, that you really are working, learning anything about how to write—

Interviewer: Yeah.

Carol: More for people who are having problems.

Allen: Yeah, I agree. It was for people that, that didn't know how, how to get to that final draft, but if you could do it on your own, you were screwed.

(pause)

Interviewer: Okay.

Jane: Didn't he say that if your notebook was really good, he'd look at that more, and if your papers were really good he'd look at—

Allen: No.

Jane: Those papers more?

Allen: He really didn't—

[General class disagreement]

Allen: Did he? I don't know. I must've been gone.

[Laughter]

Arthur: Well, I, I was writing the same way where I'd write the first draft and, uh, I'd hand that in, but then, doing some of the stuff I say, I'd say it did help. Especially that audience analysis thing, I never did that before, and, um, I <u>did</u> have to change a lot of my form and stuff like that in order to try to <u>get</u> the grades, I wanted the grade, but I think that <u>helped</u> me too, that audience analysis thing, I think that was the <u>biggest</u> that I learned out of here. Um, I didn't, I'm not going to change a lot of my writing techniques, I don't think you can, you can show some new ideas, but not necessarily change them, you can do—you <u>could,</u> uh, <u>add</u> those things, I never knew about writing, different writing techniques, I just wrote the way I write. I probably still <u>will,</u> but sometimes I'll use those kind of things, you know—because a tree, use an outline, and that, uh, audience thing I use it all the time now, I did do that for like history class and stuff like that and it works.

(pause)

Interviewer: So. You feel like maybe the strategies that Allen feels like you, um, were sort of forced on him, and that he didn't really need, were things that you may or may not use, but—

Arthur: They're helpful, though. I think that every, I should know what they are—

Interviewer: But the audience part of it was—

Arthur: The audience part was definitely a plus. It was.

Interviewer: Uh-hunh.

(pause)

Jacob: I guess, you know, what everybody's been trying to say so far is that I think he should have—I think what he—the fact that he taught those techniques are good and that people should know the techniques, but the fact that he <u>graded</u> upon whether they <u>used</u> them or not, I think what he should be grading on how the final drafts are, <u>not</u> whether they used the techniques or not—

Allen: Yeah, 'cause in certain cases a person <u>would use</u> that technique, and other times they wouldn't feel they would need to, you know, use it, and so I don't think they should, you know, be graded on whether they used it or not, mostly the final draft, but made sure that everybody <u>learned</u> how to use it if they needed. That's what—

Jacob: I agree.

Laura: I think it was good to supposed to be <u>aware</u> of having to think about them, but I don't—we didn't write them all down, you know, where uh, where uh—

Jacob: Seemed to be pressured into it—

Laura: Right.

Jacob: If you wanted to do it because otherwise your grade wouldn't be good—

[General agreement]

Allen: We were, we were writing papers that we thought were good, but we would have to change them for him to get the grade.

(pause)

Jeremy: Well, did you think your papers were perfect when you came in here?

Allen: Perfect?

Jeremy: I mean the whole purpose of this is to improve your writing—

Allen: Your technique is what it wound up being—

Jeremy: Yeah, improve your technique, I mean, you're saying that you didn't want to go through the process of trying to do that, you thought your writing was good enough from the start.

Allen: Good enough, but perfect, no.

(pause)

Jeremy: Well, I mean, then why not go through the processes that's going to improve it? He said it would. And that's all he wants you to do.

Allen: Yeah, I know but—

Arthur: I think the grading was confusing, I think we're, that's where I got unglad—

Unidentified female student: Right.

Arthur: I just don't, you know, I'm not, I'd say everything that I learned in here, I'm not, not mad I did it, you know, I'm, I think it helped me but I was so confused I'm, uh, I still don't know, I don't have any idea what I'm going to get in this class—

[General laughter]

Arthur: I hand in the notebook, and—

[General laughter]

Interviewer: What, what kind of effect does that have on you?

(pause)

Arthur: It—I, you know, you would think that it would make you work harder, but, that's not always necessarily true either. I—I don't know—

Interviewer: Could you—

Arthur: I, I got a C, I got a C+ on mine too, I think everyone got a C+—

Jeremy: I don't think so—

[Noise and general laughter]

Jeremy: I don't think those grades were that important, I mean, basically the way I think he's going to look at your final work.

Susan: I don't, because—

Jeremy: Because, what'd he say, 67 percent—

Susan: 67 percent is your notebook, I mean—

Kris: And that <u>includes</u> your final papers.

(pause)

Jeremy: He's going to look, I mean, when I talked to him he said he'd rather grade on improvement than he would on your work. So like he, if you take, if he does, really does good on you he'll look at how you started writing, then he'll look at your final papers, and he'll grade on that purpose, but no one's sure <u>how</u> he's going to do that. I mean he says he is, but that doesn't mean he is, I mean if—

(pause)

Jeremy: I mean you really don't know exactly what he's going to do, he said he'd <u>like</u> to but that doesn't mean he's going to.

(pause)

Susan: Another thing is when I'm all confused, was looking through my notebook and all the things that he wrote that I didn't have, he goes "Where are all these things" and I didn't think that I had to go back from the first week of class and do all these things in the notebook that you were doing that one, and he said that your notebook would get a lot off if you didn't do that, and he never told the class and that. Well I told my group and that—we all did it.

Bill: Did you go back?

Susan: He said he expected it—

Jeremy: Yeah, he told us to do it.

Susan: Did he? 'Cause he didn't tell the class.

Allen: Go back and do what? You—

Susan: All you were missing, I mean, everything that you missed you had to do it all.

(pause)

Interviewer: So there sounds like there was a certain amount of confusion about grading, um, was that, was that confusion about, um, what would <u>earn</u> a good grade? or was it confusion about what the grades <u>meant</u>, or what?

Stacy: Both. All of that. [laughs] A lot of confusion.

Interviewer: Lot of confusion.

Laura: You know, and he would, and he would tell you all the good papers that I'm giving you grades on, aren't really what matters, only the last one matters? Well, if it's only the last one that matters—

Unidentified male student: Why do you grade them?

Laura: then why the grade? Yeah, what, what does the grade mean then?
Interviewer: Um-hmm.

(pause)

Jane: They give you an idea of where you're at.
Unidentified female student: I didn't think that, you know, <u>how</u> I did—
Arthur: I didn't have any idea.
Stacy: He may give you—
Unidentified male student: Did you know where you were at?
Stacy: a grade higher—
Arthur: I didn't.
Stacy: anyway.

(pause)

Jeremy: Well basically the whole comp department has a poor system of grading because it's all dependent on the teacher's, um—
Allen: Point of view.
Jeremy: point of view. Um—
Allen: I mean—
Jeremy: Your writing could be good for one teacher, for another teacher could be terrible. Just up to the instructor you have. And so I mean, basically you have to shape your writing to fit the instructor, no matter if your writing's good or not.
Laura: I think that—least from talking to other people who live on my floor and my friends, there doesn't seem to be any <u>unity</u> in the comp department. One friend of mine got <u>totally</u> different, not done any of the tagmemics or any of the things we've done. She writes on all personal subjects that they—
Unidentified female student: Yeah.
Laura: that are her own, nothing that she ever had to really think about. Another friend of mine, totally different on the other, you know, from both of ours.
Interviewer: How do you feel about that?
Laura: I think—
Interviewer: I mean, if—
Laura: it's a real <u>mess.</u>
Interviewer: You think that's bad?
Laura: I think I could have gone into Kate's class and been able to write you know things that were very familiar to me and just whip them off and do <u>better</u> than I'm doing in <u>here</u>—
Interviewer: Right.

(pause)

Laura: And so to me it just doesn't seem right, I just—

Interviewer: So, you think the discrepancy's bad, if you had the <u>choice,</u> which class do you think would be more the one you <u>need?</u>

(pause)

Laura: Probably this one.

(pause)

Unidentified male student: What about—

Laura: Makes you work more, I mean, he tells us—

Interviewer: What, what about it makes you really—you feel you got out of it that you needed that the other class still wouldn't provide?

Laura: Well, like what he was talking about on Monday where no two— we were trying to write more professionally, more, uh, create a flyer, what <u>Kate</u> is going through is just, you know, here's my paper on all experience how—or this writer and this is more specialized.

(pause)

Arthur: What about those labs, too, because I got confused there, um, he said we only had to go to like four of them. I talked to a couple other people who went, and they used labs in their classes a lot more. I don't know if he covered all the stuff, um, in this class that the labs had, I looked through some of them, lab notes—except every time I went to the lab I didn't like it, they just read right through the paper that they handed out. I just stopped going, 'cause I, I, if I wanted to I could read through the paper. That's all there was to it.

Interviewer: Well, I think some, some instructors have required attendance—

Unidentified female student: I know.

Interviewer: And Robert doesn't. But—

Arthur: Okay, but I think the labs—

Interviewer: You can—

Arthur: For when I went the, you know, about six times, I didn't like it. I don't think it was, I mean it was just reading through every paper.

(pause)

Interviewer: I'm interested in the comment that was made about the, the whole, that, that in order to work through the comp program here, what you got to do is figure out what the instructor wants. All right.

[General class assent]

Jacob: Yeah. Yeah. Um, see if I can interject right here that, um, I, that's true in just about any um, comp class, and everybody kind of knows that I suppose, but his instructions were very unclear too—

Interviewer: Whose?

Susan: Yeah.

Jacob: Um, Robert's. Robert Brooke. They were real unclear as to what he really wanted you to do in the assignment, and we'd just, you know, half the time he'd give us the assignment and everybody just sat there blindly—

[General laughter]

Jeremy: In all the classes—

Jacob: You know.

Jeremy: you can talk to anyone, I mean, they just say "write a paper," they don't give them a topic, any commands, they just say "write a paper," and you just get to—

(pause)

Interviewer: What, what was that?

Jeremy: You don't find a lot in other classes—

Interviewer: In other classes.

Jeremy: Like my friends, I mean, you know, they, the teacher just says "write a paper," "write a five page paper"—

Kris: In all—

Jeremy: It's due, whenever, I mean they don't give them a topic or anything like that they just say "write a paper."

Kris: Shouldn't all the comp classes be taught the same, I mean don't they have a certain something to follow? Each comp class? I mean, no one else, all my friends they never did all the stuff that we do.

(pause)

Kris: Don't they—

Interviewer: How do you feel about that?

Kris: don't they have a certain format to follow, that they <u>have</u> to use some stuff and—

Interviewer: There are some fundamental goals within which instructors have a fair amount of license.

(pause)

Interviewer: And some of them experiment.

Jeremy: What is the purpose of this comp department for, um, freshman comp?

(pause)

Interviewer: What do <u>you</u> think it is? What, what <u>should</u> it be, maybe we should talk about that?

Jeremy: Um, to improve your writing, to help you better your technique and not basically to grade your final papers. I mean, 'cause, I mean, it should grade your improvement, really like he says he's going to do, 'cause I mean, I don't know why, what's the difference I mean, like you're going to take another class later on, but I mean if they improve your writing in this class, then you'll be able to write better, but I don't see what, the importance, you know, of—

(pause)

Allen: Or what if, Jeremy, you know the method and you don't improve.

(pause)

Jeremy: Well—

Arthur: I think the purpose is—

Laura: Well I think you've got to be open to improvement before you can improve.

Jeremy: I don't know if there's anyone in freshman comp who's good enough that they can say they can do that.

Laura: You can't go into it with a closed mind, and say "that's it."

(pause)

Arthur: I think the purpose of this class was to, uh, break you away from high school writing, high school English writing, into the college forms because I know my English stuff was just all grammar, um, its, it was really, you know, whatever, whatever you want to do is fine, you know, it didn't look at any other points, um, purely how you wrote and who you were writing to. It just looked at grammar. How it was set up. You used big words in there and stuff like that, um, that was, that was what was different here, that's what I thought real interesting is the big change, how like instructors look at writing.

Carol: [long inaudible passage]

Lars: I think a lot of the class was finding out on yourself and that's why he seemed vague a lot of the time. You know, he was trying to teach you by letting you figure it out yourself. Doesn't tell you a lot, the assignments seem vague and then you do it and you find out about [inaudible]. And that's his method of teaching which I think it worked for me. I don't know.

Interviewer: How so? What'd it do for you? What'd you find out?

Lars: Well, like on the first assignment, you know writing for two audiences, you know—Sure, that sounds just fine, and then you sit down and you do it, find out well, for two audiences you write two distinct things, well if he just told me that, I'd say "Well, yeah sure. You know, we'll" and I'd close right in. Now, I won't know exactly what that means, I know, I'd know that if I write for one audience, you know, I just found out and, like with every assignment I found something else like that out, you know, it sank in, and I, you know, I know exactly what he was trying to get across to us.

Interviewer: So if I—so for example you'd say if I decided to try to teach this same course but stood up in the front of the room for the first three weeks and said "these are the things you need to do" and then for the next five, six, seven weeks let everybody practice those things it probably wouldn't work as well?

Lars: Yeah.

Interviewer: Is that what you're saying?

Lars: I guess so.

Laura: Well I think your least duty is to tell the class, um, right away, uh, what the main expectation of the course is. You know, what—this is what I want you to try to learn and try to—

Interviewer: Uh-hunh.

Laura: You know, get from this class.

Interviewer: What, what do you think the main objective or goal of this class was?

Laura: To improve.

Stacy: Like that, the thing he showed us Monday with the freshmen versus the experienced writers, he should have showed us that right away. "It's probably where you're at," you know, "if you're this far, you know with freshman writing, and this is where you should be"—

Unidentified female student: We hope you are—

Stacy: Yeah. "Where you should be by the end of this course" and <u>then</u> go through the different assignments—

Interviewer: Um-hmm.

Stacy: And then.

Interviewer: Okay. If, if, uh, if you were going to <u>advise</u> somebody about what to change, what to keep, what things would fall in what category? (pause)

Interviewer: What's the one thing you wouldn't take out of this class?

Jane: Conference groups.

Interviewer: The conference groups?

Laura: Once you're in one.

Interviewer: Is that generally?—

(pause)

Carol: No. I feel I could have done without the conference group. We had four people to start with, and then one girl dropped, and then, uh, the two other people in my conference group never helped me at all and then the guy dropped, and the last girl, I don't know—

Stacy: Maybe, maybe you should have asked him if you could, like sit in on another one?

Carol: [long inaudible passage]

Interviewer: Um-hmm.

(pause)

Interviewer: Anything else that, that, uh, anybody else have any other ideas about what, what they'd keep?

Arthur: The audience analysis stuff like that.

Unidentified female student: Yeah.

Arthur: I liked that. I thought that helped.

Unidentified female student: Yeah.

Interviewer: Is that a general—

[General assent]

Interviewer: Pretty much?

(pause)

Interviewer: There was some allusion to figuring out what, um, instructors want, what'd Robert want?

(pause)

Interviewer: I mean, conceivably some of you figured it out, right?

(pause)

[laughter]

Stacy: Not me!

[laughter]

Interviewer: Or is Robert just <u>really good</u> at hiding what it is he wants?

Lars: I think he really just wanted improvement in each of us, I mean I don't think he wanted any particular kind of writing as long as we improved.

(pause)

Interviewer: What's, what do you mean by "improve"?

(pause)

Lars: That, you know, to be writing like he said for a college, you know, level audience, you know. Be concerned about your audience, um, be writing in a different style for college.

(pause)

Interviewer: Okay.

(pause)

Interviewer: What would you get rid of?

(pause)

[nervous laughter]

(pause)

Interviewer: What would you change?

Lars: The labs.

Interviewer: The class? How?

Carol: No, the labs.

Interviewer: Oh, the labs. Okay the Tuesday-Thursday?

Carol: Um-hmm.

Interviewer: Okay.

(pause)

Interviewer: Anything else about the class? Particularly?

Jane: I can't remember all the things.

Arthur: I still think it might have been better on some of the papers if I had a better idea what the assignment was—maybe not what I had to do with it, but what it was. Exactly, I mean, you know, how, what you should include in your paper, you know, not give away what the purpose of the, what the purpose of the paper was, but explain what the paper, what you were supposed to do in the paper. 'Cause that was, kind of procrastinated for a week before I got started because I couldn't figure it out—

Laura: Just trying to figure out what was going on—

Arthur: You know, what was going on, you know. I could have been writing, you know, two weeks. Small parts on how to do stuff, you know, that's where I got lost, kind of confused.

Stacy: Then I think after we turn in a paper for every time we have conference group and to Brooke and, and then, they gave it back to us and said "Well, this, this, this is wrong." Great. That's nice. And then you'd toss it aside and go on to the next project, you know, maybe we should have, you know, tried to revise each project 'cause by that time when we'd meet in our conference groups, and we'd looked at each others' papers, by that time we'd pretty well figured out what the assignment was—

Laura: Yeah.

Stacy: You know, so then we could revise it knowing what the assignment was supposed to have been.

Interviewer: Okay.

Laura: And I think that would lessen the jitters, I would get so frustrated. Given feedback, I might have worked on it, and it was so off what he wanted you to do, you know, that I wouldn't get a good grade, then I felt bad. You could, you could just get yourself in a hole and said, "Well, you know, if I'm never going to do the assignment right I'm not going to bother putting any effort into it—"

Interviewer: Um-hmm.

Laura: It was just like, where am I going?

(pause)

Jane: I felt like I wasted a lot of time writing papers that wasn't what he wanted. We'd get in conference groups and he'd tell me how to totally change it. And I'd wasted all that time on the paper that wasn't it.

Interviewer: What did he want?

Jane: Mostly wanted a purpose and an audience. Most of the assignments were too difficult—

Laura: Well, I think a lot of the time—

Jane: If he could have told us—

Laura: Then we could—if he had told us then we could have gone on you know and really practiced it, rather than just said "Oh. Okay. That's what you wanted." And just walking away.

Stacy: Yeah, if we'd have, if we'd have then revised it knowing what he wanted, you know—

Arthur: Right. The revision helped but the original draft—

Stacy: Yeah.

Arthur: I, a lot of times I just blew it because I had no idea that I was supposed to write to an audience really, in that specific thing. You know, I just—I handed it in and then all of a sudden I just got audience analysis on every one of my papers, I mean it, everything I got. So. When I re-write, when I rewrote them, it was better. But that's all I got. "Better." I didn't get, you know, improved this much or that much, I just "Better."

George: [laughs]

Interviewer: Did you think it was better?

Arthur: It was. I thought it was better in the sense of looking at it if I—when I concentrated on the audience. Overall, I mean, I wrote most of them, I don't know, maybe in a general sense to everyone, you can pick your own audience, you know.

(pause)

Arthur: But specifically, yes, it was better form. Which I guess you have to write that way for college anyway. [laughs]

(pause)

Interviewer: Okay. Is that pretty much it? Anybody got any more—

Carol: [inaudible statement]
Interviewer: Okay. Last thoughts?
(pause)
Jacob: It wasn't as bad as it seemed really. It was, you learned some stuff, you just, I think you got frustrated—
Kris: [inaudible]
Interviewer: What was that?
Kris: I said he didn't mean to discourage you, just to flunk you.
[laughter]
Interviewer: Um. Okay. Now I handed out some paper—(tape ends).

Works Cited

Annas, P. 1985. Style as politics: A feminist approach to the teaching of writing. *College English* 47:360–79.

Aronowitz, S., and H. Giroux. 1985. *Education under seige: The conservative, liberal and radical debate over schooling.* South Hadley, MA: Bergin and Garvey.

Bereiter, C. 1980. "Development in writing." In *Cognitive processes in writing,* ed. L. Gregg and E. Steinberg. Hillsdale, NJ: Erlbaum.

Bizzell, P. 1982. Cognition, convention, and certainty: What we need to know about writing. *Pre/Text* 3:213–44.

———. 1984. William Perry and liberal education. *College English* 46: 447–54.

———. 1988. Arguing about literacy. *College English* 50:141–53.

Brooke, R. 1987. Underlife and writing instruction. *College Composition and Communication* 38:141–53.

———. 1988. Modeling a writer's identity: Reading and imitation in the writing classroom. *College Composition and Communication* 39:23–41.

Calkins, L. 1983. *Lessons from a child.* Portsmouth, NH: Heinemann.

Ede, L. 1984. Audience: An introduction to research. *College Composition and Communication* 35:140–54.

Ede, L., and A. Lunsford. 1984. Audience addressed/audience invoked: The role of audience in composition theory and pedagogy. *College Composition and Communication* 35:155–71.

Elbow, P. 1981. *Writing with power.* New York: Oxford UP.

Erikson, E. 1950. *Childhood and society.* New York: Norton.

———. 1968. *Identity, youth, and crisis.* New York: Norton.

Flower, L. 1979. Writer-based prose. *College English* 41:19–37.

———. 1985. *Problem solving strategies for writing*. 2nd ed. New York: Harcourt Brace Jovanovich.

Flower, L. et al. 1986. Detection, diagnosis, and the strategies of revision. *College Composition and Communication* 37:16–55.

Freire, P. 1970. *Pedagogy for the oppressed*. New York: Continuum.

———. 1973. *Education for critical consciousness*. New York: Seabury.

Giroux, H. 1981. *Ideology, culture, and the process of schooling*. Philadelphia: Temple UP.

———. 1983. *Theory and resistance in education*. Boston: Bergin and Garvey.

Goffman, E. 1961. *Asylums: Essays on the social situation of mental patients and other inmates*. New York: Anchor.

———. 1963. *Stigma: Notes on the management of spoiled identity*. Englewood Cliffs, NJ: Prentice-Hall.

———. 1967. *Interaction ritual: Essays on face-to-face behavior*. New York: Pantheon.

Heath, S. B. 1982. Ethnography in education: Defining the essentials. In *Ethnography and education: Children in and out of school*, ed. P. Gilmore and A. Glatthorn, 33–55. Washington, DC: Center for Applied Linguistics.

———. 1983. *Ways with words*. New York: Cambridge UP.

Kantor, K. 1984. Classroom contexts and the development of writing intentions: An ethnographic case study. In *New directions in composition research*, ed. R. Beach and L. Bridwell, 72–94. New York: Guilford.

Kantor, K., D. Kirby, and J. Goetz. 1981. Research in context: Ethnographic studies in English education. *Research in the Teaching of English* 15:293–309.

Labov, W. 1972. *Language in the inner city*. Philadelphia: Pennsylvania UP.

Laing. R.D. 1960. *The divided self*. New York: Pantheon.

———. 1961. *Self and others*. New York: Pantheon.

———. 1967. *The politics of experience*. New York: Pantheon.

———. 1982. *The voice of experience*. New York: Pantheon.

Laing, R. D., and A. Esterson. 1970. *Sanity, madness, and the family: Families of schizophrenics*. 2nd ed. New York: Basic Books.

Lauer, J., et al. 1981. *Four worlds of writing*. New York: Harcourt Brace Jovanovich.

Lunsford, A. 1979. Cognitive development and the basic writer. *College English* 41:39–46.

Marcus, G., and M. Fischer. 1986. *Anthropology as cultural critique: An experimental moment in the human sciences.* Chicago: Chicago UP.

Mitchell, R., and M. Taylor. 1979. The integrating perspective: An audience-response model for writing. *College English* 41:247–71.

North, S. 1986. Writing in a philosophy class: Three case studies. *Research in the Teaching of English* 20:225–62.

Perry, W. 1970. *Forms of intellectual and ethical development in the college years.* New York: Holt.

Piaget, J. 1950. *Introduction a l'epistemologie genetique.* 3 vols. Paris: France UP.

Rose, M. 1985. The language of exclusion: Writing instruction at the university. *College English* 47:341–59.

Rouse, J. 1985. Scenes from the writing workshop. *College English* 47: 217–36.

Sommers, N. 1980. Revision strategies of student writers and experienced adult writers. *College Composition and Communication* 31:378–87.

Willis, P. 1977. *Learning to labour: How working class kids get working class jobs.* Lexington, MA.: D.C. Heath.

Young, R., A. Becker, and K. Pike. 1970. *Rhetoric: Discovery and change.* New York: Harcourt Brace Jovanovich.

Robert Brooke grew up in Denver, Colorado, and attended Gonzaga University and the University of Minnesota. He is now an assistant professor at the University of Nebraska-Lincoln, where he serves as co-coordinator of composition and participates in the Nebraska Writing Projects. His essays have appeared in *College English* and *College Composition and Communication,* and he received the 1988 Braddock Award for his article "Underlife and writing instruction."

John Hendricks was born in Chattahoochee County, Georgia, attended St. Olaf College, Iowa State University, and the University of Minnesota. Between 1982 and 1985 he taught in the University of Minnesota Program in Composition and Communication. In 1985 he made a career shift and entered medical school. He is currently an intern at the University of Minnesota Medical School.